The Extra Lesson

by Audrey E. McAllen

Wilfred Marfield
25·5·1987

Exercises in Movement, Drawing and Painting
for helping Children in difficulties with
Writing, Reading and Arithmetic

Steiner Schools Fellowship Publications

ISBN 0 9510331 0 7

First printed October 1974
Second edition (revised) 1980
German translation 1982; Spanish translation 1984
Third edition (revised and re-organised) . . .1985
Reprinted . . .1986
Published by
Steiner Schools Fellowship Publications, Michael Hall School
Forest Row, East Sussex, RH18 5 JB, United Kingdom

Printed by
Imprint Publicity Service, Sussex, England

DEDICATION

To the memory of
FREDERICK GEUTER
who introduced me to the life work
of Rudolf Steiner
and made me want to become an educator

ACKNOWLEDGEMENTS

My warm thanks go to. . .

Miss Else Göttgens, Holland, for permission to publish her exercises based on the relationship between the senses: The Rod Rolling and Counting Star Exercises, and the "Rhythmic Reading" Technique; The Editor of the Rudolf Steiner Nachlassverwaltung, Dornach, Switzerland, for permission to include an exercise by Rudolf Steiner; The late Dr. Maria Glas, M.D. (Vienna), who showed me "The Grand Crawl".

Arthur Osmond, Michael Hall School, Sussex, for editing, illustrating and helping to reorganise this edition; Olive Tapp, who typed the first edition, and Joyce Russell, who proof-read both editions; Margaret Shillan, who designed the cover, and Peter Ramm for the illustration on the cover; Anne McNicol for her precise typesetting and helpful comments.

E. C. Byford, for his tireless work over many years as publisher and distributor for The Steiner Schools Fellowship, U.K.

A. E. M., Tuffley, Gloucester, 1985

LIST OF ILLUSTRATIONS

CONTENTS

FOREWORD

This book is a delight, and it was with immense pleasure that I accepted the invitation to write its Foreword.

There is a secret in the book which will stay hidden if it is read as a book about problems and how they can be solved, for this is something which can only be understood by 'doing' and thus discovering the secret. If the reader himself 'does' the exercises, he will find he is entering into the heart of the matter; something which is the central question for everyone, namely, the chapter on "How do I get into my body?".

In the pedagogical lectures given by Rudolf Steiner, he points repeatedly to the development of the small child during the first three years. If you can involve yourself intensively in these processes, they can then become a key to understanding the soul of the child. If in these first three years even slight injuries occur, i.e. trauma during the birth-processes, illness, accidents, tensions in the family, they can all have repercussions in the child's further development. This shows itself when he enters school and learning and/or behavioural difficulties become apparent.

The assessments described in "The Extra Lesson" are, by virtue of their simplicity, a great help in diagnosing and localising the possible problems. If we want to help the child, we have to begin in those areas where the disturbances first started.

The exercises indicated in this book show us the way. Development processes are undergone once more, and the child can take himself into his own body again. This clears the way for him to develop true interest for learning. To witness the joy which the child shows in these circumstances is something I would wish every teacher to experience. "The Extra Lesson" makes this possible.

Claartje Wijnbergh

The Tobias School for Children
with Learning Difficulties

Amsterdam, 1985

INTRODUCTION

Education rests on the development of faculty. Today we are faced with more and more children who are not able to unfold the basic requirements in writing, reading and arithmetic, thus seriously limiting their reception of education as provided today.

As teachers we impart our knowledge, we are pleased when it is reflected back to us in an original way; as educators we have to ask what faculty does our subject matter produce and what effect does our method of teaching have on the health and bodily development of our pupils. Looking over a set of writing books from children aged 6 − 8 years, the teaching eye in us will be pleased when it sees beautifully written work, displeased at badly formed, untidy, grubby work. But our educating eye will make us pause and think: "Is this neatness and ability too precise for the age of the child? Is there a danger of a lapse at about 9 years when a change comes about in the relationship between the child's experience of himself and his environment?* Will such a pupil present us with 7 or 8 pages of repetitive description when he is 12 years old? And the clumsy work, does it conceal an ability to describe an experience in a few graphic words or is the bodily development so difficult that the faculties will be drowned in it, and lethargy, discouragement and emotional attitudes develop?".

If we, as educators, have not been able to draw forth faculty, then we have to ask, "Have the experiences through which these faculties should be developed not been wide enough, or have they not been brought to the child at the right age?".

The methods of work developed by the writer are concerned with finding educational means to help the child unfold whatever faculty is possible and appropriate to his age. An education founded on the Spiritual Scientific Research of Rudolf Steiner takes as its basic premise the process set up between the individuality's soul/spirit and those aspects (physical body and life-body) offered through the heredity of the parents. These two composite members of every human being have a living, fluctuating relationship resembling the breathing process of inhalation and exhalation. This principle is worked out in detail in Steiner's 'Waldorf School' pedagogy. The learning problems which the normal child is now encountering are specific instances of when this 'breathing process' is not in order.

---

* König, K. *The First Three Years of the Child,* Chapter 4
  Brown, C. *My Left Foot,* Chapters 3 − 4

For example, the physical body can have been interfered with by the side-effects of drugs, tranquillizers, anti-pain injections and other environmental circumstances, or the individuality may not be strong enough in his soul/spirit to master the type of heredity which the parental constitution offers.

These factors require us to look closely at the physical body in its structural organisation of skeleton, muscles, nerves, and at the time when the soul/spirit of the individuality is entering into the closest connection of their development — namely the time from birth to the change of teeth, which occurs between 6 to 7 years.

This structural, physical body which is offered to the soul/spiritual individual through the stream of heredity is the work during previous aeons of time of the Creator Spirits of the Universe. Hence all skeletons have the same archetypal construction, our muscles are attached to it in the same places and are organised to lift and move it, and our nerves to sense its response in relation to perception. This is a fact common to all humanity; our responses are, of course, individual, but structurally we share the same 'archetypal physical body' which is a spatial organ for the consciousness of our individuality as we live and move on the planet earth.

In an important lecture-cycle entitled *Anthroposophy* (given in Berlin in 1909), Steiner lays the basis for his concepts of the senses, the interconnection between man's supersensible organisation and that of the planet earth, and the results of the directions of writing on our soul constitutions. It is in these lectures that he gives us a fundamental law in relation to the movements between the astral (soul) body and the physical and ether (life) bodies, of which the nerves, muscles and skeleton are the physical manifestation of these supersensible organs.*

Steiner states that the astral body moves in the opposite direction to that of the physical/life bodies, and he further relates these to the movements of the supersensible members of the earth planet itself.

This is one of the keys to understanding the spatial-movement problems of the child, which is basic to the movement exercises in this book. Another spiritual scientific fact is that the movement of our soul (astral) through the physical/life bodies during the day is a clockwise spiral.

We can see the inter-relation between the spatial organisation of the physical body which the ego of the child lifts into three dimensional space when he stands upright and the spiral of the soul if we notice the spatial

---

* See: Steiner, R. *Occult Science — An Outline*, Chapter 2.
  Schumacher, *Guide to the Perplexed*. (For a dialectical description of these supersensible organs.) Sphere Books Ltd., London, 1978

properties of the spiral in movement. As we draw it, we move from above to below, from left to right, from outside to inside. We can see the inter-relationship of these spatial movements of space and spiral in craftwork and domestic movements, e.g. weaving, spinning, stirring, wringing out washing, etc., all activities which bring to birth intelligence, as anyone engaged in Steiner's Waldorf education will know.

These two premises, together with the fact that it is in the 'gap' between the sensory and the perceptive motor nerves — the synapse — where we are inter-penetrated by the spiritual world that justifies the necessity for movement, drawing and painting exercises to be so composed that these spiritual scientific laws are taken into account. A right relationship to the 'breathing' between the soul/spirit of the incarnating individuality and his life/physical body can be re-established.

Furthermore, this space in which we stand, although 'empty' to our senses in daytime, is, in reality, penetrated by moral forces which support and nourish our soul/spiritual being. It is in these moral forces that we live during sleep, hence our movement exercises bring us also in relationship to these as they spiritually underly those of our planet's own supersensible movements into which we enter during sleep.

The content of this book is a first attempt at the correlation of these spiritual scientific facts with the problems presented by the child with learning difficulties.

Chapter One

THE DEVELOPMENT OF MOVEMENT
IN THE FIRST SEVEN YEARS

The first awakening to the physical body, the first experience the baby has of his 'body-geography', comes when he leaves the womb and starts the journey through the birth canal. He is seized by the expansion and contraction of his mother's muscles, a rhythm which massages his whole body and stimulates the nerves which have their focus in the brain stem. Every one of our senses has within it the element of touch and in these hours of his mother's labour the sum total of all the senses — which are the manifestation of the physical body — are brought into play ready to co-ordinate at the supreme moment when the air outside rushes into the lungs and baby lives. The strength of the first cry is of great importance as it is from the intake of the breath that the blood, for the first time, is forced to flow through the lungs, the air sacs expand and this in turn closes the valve (foramen ovale) between the two chambers of the heart. The three vessels of the umbilical cord seal off, and the whole lower system of the liver, spleen, kidneys and their reflexes is activated. All this takes place in a matter of seconds. It is no wonder that there has always been an emphasis and concern for baby's first cry. The work of the individuality during his sojourn in the womb, creating a body able to bear life and consciousness, culminates in this moment.

It is not so much birth-trauma that causes problems at a later time, (after all babies have been born in all situations and difficult conditions down the centuries). What is different now is the welter of sense impressions which pour onto them from the day of birth onwards: noise, radio, T.V., people coming and going, the vacuum cleaner buzzing around the cot, lights switching on and off, the thumping and rushing of the washing machine. How different this is to the rhythmic beat of mother's heart and the gentle surging of her blood-circulation which modern investigations tell us are heard by the baby in the uterus.

Compare the type of noises in today's households with the, not so long ago, Victorian environment of the nursery, with its drawn blinds for the first days, very few visits until the christening six weeks later, and then a quiet regime with brothers and sisters who were allowed only 'peeps' for a few minutes until baby was old enough to lift his head himself.

Such observations are not advocating a return to past standards, habits and manners, but rather to suggest that parenthood is our highest profession and requires much more knowledge, training and thought than we at present allocate to it. A thorough understanding of the child's development as a spiritual being opens up quite new and exciting concepts and possibilities for being creative in so many ways, and lifts nappy-changing into quite another context! Replanning one's home and lifestyle does not mean rearranging one's life round the baby and being its slave, but instead making conscious decisions rather than saying, "Oh, the baby must learn to fit in with us" — a demand we would hardly make on an adult.

This peace of the Victorian era allowed for physiological and soul adjustments to take place. The skull bones, tightly compressed by the passage through the birth canal, have to loosen and expand so that the complicated processes of the cell growth of the brain structure can take place, the cranial pulse can establish itself, and the head can attain the lovely rounded dome that pictures the cosmos from which the soul has come. (The head of the baby is as busy as a beehive in its growth and development.) The steady pace of baby's daily life was a healing process in itself. The modern baby is seldom allowed this calm in which to recuperate from the strenuous effort of birth, and the time to live into his organism undisturbed by our mechanized and demanding routines.

As an observant mother commented, "After a few days of quiet and calm, babies are happier, cheerful, more centred and outgoing. They seem to have a realization of where they are. When they have days where too much is happening around them they are irritable and fractious".

During the first months of his life the baby will spend his days lying on his back. It is from this horizontal position that he will reach out with his senses into his surroundings, his eyes following his mother round the room and turning them towards the direction of the sounds he hears. He needs such a stable position as the point of reference for relating his experiences one to the other. If it is altered, for example by propping him on a pillow, then this point of reference for co-ordinating his perceptions is interfered with. It would be better to move the cot or pram into different places to give a variety of experience, than to change the body position prematurely. Then again, the modern habit of leaving a baby on his stomach, before he is strong enough, out of his own forces, to lift his head and roll himself over, deprives him of a free stretching and rotating of the arms into the air, the joy of fingering the sunbeams, and the absorbing interest of contemplating his hands! 'Tummy-lying' for short periods of exercise, yes, but not a lying position during the daytime.

It requires the first nine months for a baby to integrate and overcome the gravity-weight of his body. The head and upper limbs are the first to do this, giving him the capacity to roll over from side to side through lifting his head. Alas, in how many instances is the baby denied the experience of raising his head himself? Long before the muscles are ready to support his head, he is held upright too frequently, for too long at a time, or falls asleep in a 'chest carrier' his head lolling back with the weight of the skull resting on the shoulders, pushing the neckbones out of alignment.

These nine months are the time when the head and arms are the means by which the baby moves himself, carrying his weight. This time can be shortened by encouraging him to use the lower limbs as weight-bearing organs — by helping him on to his legs with walking aids or sitting him upright in babywalkers or babybouncers; we are putting him prematurely into the vertical position and depriving him of the time he needs to develop control of the posture of his body, and the natural co-ordinating of percepts and movements which should be developed in the horizontal position*.

It is indeed a dramatic moment when the baby, out of his own forces, can co-ordinate all his muscles and lift his body upright into space and take his first steps on this earth. It is a mighty achievement. The 'lifting man' who overcomes gravity announces the unique position of the human being in the scheme of created beings. He is free to move in space, to the right — to the left — forward and back, to look up and down. The steps to this achievement of his human stature are all important to the body's capacity to achieve faculty later. The spontaneous co-ordination between the skeletal structure, muscles and nerves, enables him in due course to handle objects, and assimilate his sense-impressions and reproduce them as is required, for example, in writing and reading.

The steps that lead to spatial orientation, i.e. the ability to stand upright in space, are 'crawling' — lying on the tummy and stretching forward one hand as he looks as it, while pressing against the floor with the inner side of the opposite foot, repeating this with the other side of the body — and 'creeping' — raising himself onto his hands and knees to move about the room. In the first of these, he 'stretches' himself into the weight-gravity of his body. The second, added to the first, appears necessary to complete the full integration of the central nervous system that reflects to us our spatial and bodily awareness.

---

*Kalinger, G., and Heil, C.L. *Basic Symmetry and Balance*

Having achieved his uprightness, baby now uses his left and right sides indiscriminately — a repetition at another level of the earlier rolling from side to side stage — in other words he goes through an ambidextrous stage. It is at this time that many parents are deceived into thinking their toddler is left-handed, and so — because no training is given (like guidance in using the right side of the body in dressing, the right arm into the coat first, right shoe on right foot first), together with confusion in nomenclature (we use the term 'right' when we mean 'correct') — many children become confused during this time and so remain in this ambidextrous state, whether they are left- or right-handers, a fact which we shall find revealed when we compare their dominance with the Handedness Assessment. This unconfirmed sidedness is also the basis of the cross-laterality that inhibits learning faculties.

Sidedness — the preferred use of one side of the body, usually attained by about 6 years — is synonymous with the unification of the two brain hemispheres. The individuality can now use them at will according to the particular kind of occupation in which he is engaged. Hence the concentration span lengthens, imagination in connection with language develops and social play begins. Prior to this development, one hemisphere was used until fatigue set in, then the other hemisphere became the functional one; in careful observation of the older child with problems we can see this still happening.

The last stage in movement development is when 'everything' moves. Growth quickens, the arms and legs attain their correct proportion to the trunk of the body, the head (once overlarge in proportion to the rest of the body) now sits poised on the shoulders, and with the arm placed over the head, the hand can take hold of the opposite ear lobe — a sign that the soul/spirit has penetrated the lower limbs and that these limbs have achieved their normal proportional growth. The child has found the way into the physical body.

This body is now the child's own possession, and the signature for this is that the milk teeth of the hereditary body are pressed out and his own individualised teeth take their place. It is around the age of 7 that the body is 'schoolripe' and the individuality of the child can expect it to produce for him the faculties which he requires to learn with — spatial orientation, movement co-ordination and the ability to be able to change his sight perception instantaneously between three-dimensional and two-dimensional space.

These elements, together with good 'body geography' and confirmed dominance are the results of the child's movement exploration in relation

4

to his body, and of his environment. By now they should be functioning at the subconscious level and therefore be at his command. They are the fruit of his first 7 years of life and the capacities which the teacher needs to draw on, if the child is to learn.

Chapter Two

HOW DO I GET INTO MY BODY?

This is the unspoken question which every child asks his parents and teachers. They give him the answer by their own movements, gestures and attitudes. These he will devotedly imitate with every movement of his own body until they are part of himself. Walking behind any mother with a 3 − 4 year old will show with what love and inner attention the child has reproduced the example he is given. Now walk behind a cluster of home-going schoolchildren. Some will be walking bouncily on the balls of the feet, heels seldom contacting the ground. Others will be stumping along on flat feet: there are bottoms which are sticking out, toes that are turned in, the movements unrhythmical. Other children will be treading firmly and confidently in a steady rhythm: these are the ones who through the strength of their individualities are gradually transforming the imitated patterns into ones expressing their own latent abilities.

When the children are submerged in the imitated movements and have not the strength to free themselves, then the body no longer fits them like a glove but becomes a frustrating burden which they have to carry around. The following assessments will give us a picture of the child's situation when he has reached this state.

How *do* we get into our bodies? We can gain some idea of this if we watch someone waking up. Suddenly we know they are awake; one has sensed an almost imperceptible movement, then they stretch themselves, lift a head or arm and probably speak. In these movements − stretching-lifting-speaking sequence − we see how the adult slips into and takes hold of his body. At the moment of birth these movements are telescoped together. In the first three years of life they follow each other in rhythmic succession. In a few seconds every morning we repeat the attainments of our first three years of life.

As soon as the baby can move his head and direct his gaze, he stretches his hands to grasp what he sees. In these stretching grasping hand movements he co-ordinates his eye with space orientation: he 'stretches' or extends his way into the world of sense percepts which surround him. (It is through taking hold of the sense world that we enter gravity and the weight element of our physical body.) He imitates form and activity. His individual responses − pain, pleasure, doubt, fear, are reflected inwardly as gestures held in his 'lifting' movement system. Each child has his own individual moment when he suceeds in overcoming gravity and can stand upright and walk forward. This is an enormous 'will' accomplishment. Through lifting, walking and dancing we assert our will over the weight of our physical body and all that has given it its form from heredity and by imitation of the environment. In 'stretching' — grasping movements and lifting movements we see the interplay between the effects of the world of the senses and the individual's capacity of 'will' as response.

A welter of sense impressions surround the child from birth; so many now are of a nature that do not belong to the natural experience of childhood. For example, there is the duplication of 'pictures' which appear and disappear without our control as in T.V. and fast driving. These problems are now being aggravated by the video process which children can use indiscriminately and, alas, by computerized teaching machines which are available now even to kindergarten departments. Such things produce strong reaction in the child's feeling; inner gestures of withdrawal can be a result. These gradually ingrain themselves as concealed 'habit-gestures' in the lifting system*, that part of the muscular system which reacts in movement to the sense impressions. The inwardly held gestures in the muscles act as an obstruction to integrated movement. The child senses this frustration of his will and tries to find a way through them by adroit avoidance or compensation — cross dominances — left-sidedness — psychological protests may result until finally failures of faculty development bring attention to his predicament. The overstress of the 'stretching' movements through our present style of living, the psychological drive for early intellectual attainment which relies on sensory co-ordination and quick response, all affect the development of the spatial relationships and their internal correspondence of convex and concave mirroring in which the will of the child should actively take part.

We see these convex-concave reflections projected in the child's writing — in his reversal and the rotating of the letters. Let us look how these mirroring effects are present in every-day use. We use convex linear mirroring when we describe a landscape to a person — we give directions of position according to our own left and right — just as our own reflection appears in a mirror or on the *back* of a spoon as we hold it in front of us. But if a person stands in the landscape holding a basket, then we say in which hand he holds it according to our own right hand and his — here we cross over in our looking: this is 'concave' lens mirroring in three

---

* See observations on the Crawl Exercises, page 30

dimensional space. Now turn over the spoon, and we have a surprise: right-hand is mirrored on our left, left on the right, but we are upside down! Man's visual will-force appears to be capable of righting the sense picture, at least in three-dimensional space. When we come to two-dimensional space, that is when we place the spoon at right angles on a sheet of paper, then the concave situation is further complicated — at the centre of our spoon, form and movement are copied (not 'reflected') and are not upside down, but on the bevelled part of the spoon a drawn straight line suddenly divides into left and right.

We are constantly employed in transforming these two- and three-dimensional convex-concave relationships by movements of inner will into the content of our life of thought and feeling: as adults we do this successfully, but when complicated sense impressions have overwhelmed the growing child we see the results of his struggles to cope with them when he cannot reproduce the convex-concave 'will activity' correctly in two-dimensional space, i.e. turns the letters upside down and reverses sequences as in the Dyslexia syndrome.

Hence it is meaningful when a line is drawn vertically on paper; this is an adaptation to two-dimensional space. It brings about an immediate left-right situation. When a line is drawn horizontally we have divided space into above-below; both are convex situations. But when the diagonal line is used then the dual nature of the concave situation arises in which an activity of the will is called on to make a personal inner response, in contrast to the more passive receiving of the convex impressions. The eye in its socket can move left-right, up-down and in a circle; this we can reproduce in two dimensions. But to bring the eye into the perspective movement of near and far we have to use our limb system to carry it forward and back — the diagonal line in two-dimensional space.

When we observe the children's movements, the way in which they draw and paint, and their relation to movement when writing, we see how the over-stimulus of the 'stretching' element belonging to the apprehension of outer spatial impressions seems to press so deeply into the 'lifting' system that many of the natural movements of the 'will element' have gone into reverse.

The exercises, which will be described, themselves bring about the correct movements and directions as they are based on the child's archetypal movement-relationships between his soul/spirit and life-body/ physical body. The child discovers them through his own activity and feels strengthened in identity and confidence. On this basis faculty can then develop.

8

Chapter Three

ASSESSMENT

Types of Children with Writing, Reading and Arithmetic Problems

Slow developers: over pressurised from any source.

Quick nervous children: children who have over anxious ambitious backgrounds and reflect inwardly the anxiety of adults in their environment.

Children with emotional problems of all kinds.

Children with physiological problems: minimal brain damage. Slight spasticity in hands or legs.

Dyslexia: dominance difficulties and the attendant concave:convex mirror relationships unmastered.

Children in *all of these groups* have basic difficulties in spatial orientation, also a weakness or inability to make mental images of their sense impressions (inner visualisation).

Also complicating matters are the incomplete development stages of:

1. Discarding the positional responses;
2. Integrating co-ordination (that comes from crawling and creeping);
3. Over-coming ambidexterity;
4. Attaining good body image at the appropriate time.

The Dyslexia group add to this a lack of ability to differentiate between sounds, to recognize their symbols, and to write clearly.

The basis of writing is good eye-hand co-ordination arising from rhythmic movement. Reading, modern research tells us, comes about through minute pauses in which the rapid movements the eye makes around the forms of the letters are grasped and conceptualized; this movement of the eye involves the whole body, entering into the interaction of the nerves with the synapses and the mirroring factors between the physical-etheric and astral bodies. We must see how at home and how well organised the child is in the co-ordination of these faculties.

Assessment and Progress Tests

The following assessment and progress tests can be used for children from age 11 (unless otherwise specified for younger children) who usually come because their problems have finally come to light, or because other methods of dealing with the writing-reading difficulty have failed.

Cross Test (from 7 years)

Using loose-leaf paper suitable for filing:

(1) Ask the child to write his name on the top of the paper. Most children can manage this;

(2) Suggest he writes his address so that you get to know his writing. Some children may be able to do so. Watch the child's expression — does it become fearful or does the jaw set grimly? Be prepared to rescue the trier who gets stuck!;

(3) Ask for the date orally or written. Only very few will know this. Both town and country children have this loss of connection with the changes of time and season;

(4) Ask the child to draw a line down the centre of the paper. Tell him to put a cross on one side of it. He may ask what kind of cross: so tell him to choose the one he likes.

Observe whether the arm movement is free, or if the child moves backwards with the whole body to draw the line. On the unused side of the line we can ask him to write some spelling. If he says that he cannot spell, then spell the words for him, noting how he forms the letters, whether he joins them correctly and can distinguish the short vowel sounds. Look for reversals and for rotated letters. Examples: man, bed, pig, dog, hub, start, bread, prick, sting, jump. This will be sufficient to show the problem without discouraging the child. If he is reluctant, do not proceed. We want his energy and interest for other things.

Immediately we draw a vertical line we bring out the relationship between left and right. Which side has the child chosen? The left side shows that he is able to bring what he does into relation with what he perceives. When he places his cross on the right side of the line he shows us that he has difficulties in this respect, lapses of concentration, 'off moments', etc.

There are two kinds of crosses: St. George, vertical; St. Andrew, diagonal. The vertical cross shows that in three-dimensional space the child's visual capacity in left-right and above-below orientation is sound. He will have quick physical reaction to movement. The diagonal cross shows that he is held more in above-below orientation with slower physical reaction in movements. To characterise, the user of the vertical cross on the left side of the line will see something falling and catch it in time, but he will not necessarily assess what caused the incident. When the diagonal cross is placed on the left side, this user will see the happening and be able to explain why but he is not likely to be in time to avert the accident without a great effort of will on his part.

Most of our pupils are likely to put the cross of their choice on the right side of the line. This indicates there are obstructions coming from the organism which hinder perceptual-physical reactions. We can be very happy when children finally choose the left side of the line. This will show us our work is having an effect. It is very rare for the type of cross to be changed.

If the body has to be moved to draw the line, we may suspect some structural problem if there are further symptoms in other exercises.

Dominance

This is the using of one side of the body in preference to the other. Most of us choose the right side. We are normally right-eyed, right-handed and right-legged. Babies are ambidextrous at birth and dominance develops naturally. But careless handling or over-stimulation of the sensory organism can cause what would have been a normal right-sided dominance to vary from one side of the body to the other. For example, dominance may change from the right to the left eye or from the right to the left leg. Left-handedness is a drastic change of dominance and may be further complicated by a right-eyed and/or right-legged dominance. Mixed dominances are often found in association with reading and writing difficulties. We may help the child to change dominance of eye and leg from the left side to the right side when he is right-handed. Similarly we may help the eye and leg to change from right to left dominance if he is left-handed. *The decision for any handedness change may only be made by a doctor* and carried out under his supervision.

Simple Dominance Checks (from 7 years)

Place a rolled paper 'telescope' in front of the child and ask him to look at a picture through it and describe what he sees. Note with which hand he takes up the 'scope and the eye he chooses. Ask him to look with the other eye — does he see as much? Note how he changes the 'scope; does he take it directly to the other eye with the same hand, or does he give it to the other hand first?

Established dominance:

Right hand to right eye. . . . . or . . . . left hand to left eye;

Cross dominance:

Right hand to left eye . . . . or . . . . left hand to right eye.

11

Recheck eye dominance by asking the child to close an eye; note whether he uses his hand or can do it muscularly.

There are some children who do not appear to be able to differentiate between using one or the other eye; tell them to look through the 'scope and they do so keeping both eyes open. Ask them to look through a hole made in a postcard, to focus on a coin on the table in front of them, then to raise the postcard to their eye while keeping the coin in sight; they will, at a certain distance, stop uncertainly before taking the card to the dominant eye.

We need to strengthen the 'breathing-in' process through movement activities such as games with a 'looking-aim': skittles, throwing rings over a hook, etc. If this is not effective, then the doctor may prescribe eye exercises in Curative Eurythmy.

Foot Dominance (from 7 years)

Tell the child to stand on one leg or to stamp — there may be a cross dominance here, so check by asking him now to stand on the one leg with an eye closed. . .often the foot is changed for a moment and then the choice goes back to the original leg. This shows us that dominance from above to below is not established. The leg used to stand on is the dominant one.

Hand, Eye, Speech Co-ordination (from 7 years)

Place blue and red dyed haricot beans in a mixed pile in front of the child with one glass in front of him on his right and another on the left. Ask him to sort the beans, blue into the left glass, red into the right. Note the various methods used: (a) indiscriminate choice; (b) sorting one colour first; (c) taking a pile into a hand (note which hand); (d) changing from one hand to the other.

All this builds up a picture of the degree of uncertainty and fatigue in co-ordination. As our experience grows, a delicate perception may come of the type of gesture in these movements. Is the child holding the handful of beans in a gesture of greed or of fear? This will prepare us for the moment when the right anecdote or words of encouragement coming from us can help in his moral development.

Having sorted the beans, we can ask which colour he likes and how many of that colour there are in the glass. It is quite usual for the child to refuse to guess. Whatever the reaction is we now tip one glass out and ask him to drop them back into the glass counting out aloud. The effort to

12

speak and move will produce big sighs, showing how little strength of rhythm there is. The counting may rush ahead of the movement, or the movements overtake the speaking. Now ask how many beans he thinks there are in the other glass. The answer is usually quite out of proportion. From the performance of this activity it will be obvious whether it needs to be used as a therapy.

Handedness Pattern (relationship to 3-dimensional space: from 7 years)

For this we need two sheets of thin white card size 20 in x 30 in (55 cm x 75 cm). On one card draw a red circle as large as the card permits. On the next card we have to draw a mirror form on a horizontal axis, and on the other side a mirrored form on the vertical axis. We are now going to find out what kind of eye, hand, limb pattern the child has in relation to forms in space. A triangle was also included in this sequence but it did not add more information than that already shown by the other forms. See illustrations and assessment sheet format on pages 71 – 73.

Tell the child to take off his shoes and sit on the floor in front of the card with the circle, which is placed upright against the wall. Then tell him to let his feet follow round the circle, both feet held together: he can touch the card if he wishes. We make a note of the starting point and direction he takes. We now tell him to draw round it choosing different parts of his body in this order:

> both feet together . . . one foot. . . .foot and hand. . . .
> foot and eye. . . . . . both hands held together. . . . . . .
> one hand . . . . hand, eye. . . . .
> then to look round it with one eye covered . . . .
> Repeat this sequence with the other forms.

We make a note of the starting points on the forms (see Handedness Pattern in Appendix), direction and choice of limb. Our observations will show us that the geometrical forms are treated as circles and the symmetry forms as straight lines going forward and backward or as continuous circles, and that there is a wide discrepancy in the choice of the part of the body used, even in children with full right-handed or left-handed dominance.

An exercise to establish co-ordinated dominance and produce the correct movement pattern for the right side of the body in relation to the astral (soul) body, ether (life) body and physical body, and one for the left side will be described later – named as the Right-angle Triangle Exercise.

13

The Flower-Rod Exercise (lemniscates on a straight line : from 7 years)

This shows us if the child is able to visualise inwardly to himself the spatial dimensions. Ask the child to choose two coloured crayons and to give one to you. Sitting beside him, you or he draws a vertical line on a sheet of paper. Then, starting at the top of the line, draw one side of a lemniscate dividing the line in half. Ask him to mirror this form on the other side of the line. Most children will start as you did at the top; others will continue the line. We can then say we have made a kind of flower bulb and bud; now the sun comes and a leaf opens. Starting at the top away from the closed form draw an open-topped half lemniscate. Again the child has to mirror it. Repeat this once more. Now repeat the whole form, but starting on the right side. Finally ask the child to do it from memory.

The illustrated examples (pages 15; 82) give an idea of what may result. This is a therapy exercise as well as an assessment. In some instances it can happen that a child with a good result goes through a collapse for a time. In this beautiful form we can see if the child has the capacity to move inwardly from convex to concave mirroring and the willingness to be receptive. It also has archetypal connotations for the soul of the child (the Caduceus).

Eye-Colour Affinity (awareness of inner space : from 7 years)

So far we have been trying to find out how the child experiences his body in relation to the space outside of himself and if he is able to visualise this inwardly. Now we will try to gain an idea as to how free he is in living in his own inner relationship to space. The colours blue and red have their own objective quality – blue belongs to space which stretches out, expands and surrounds us. We experience this in the blue of the sky. Red is a colour that draws together and comes towards one, it is an active colour; blue is a passive colour. If we experience these colours inwardly our feelings are roused.

Our eyes have definite functions. The left eye is the more active in surveying space; the right eye is the one which picks out and adjusts to a specific point, as, for example, when aiming a gun at a target. Observations made by E. Lehrs in his book *Man and Matter* show that there is also an objective physiological relationship between the left eye and the colour blue and the right eye and the colour red. If a pupil is asked to make a drawing of a blue moon and a red sun some are able to do so with the colour corresponding to the left eye on the left side of the paper and

The Flower-Rod Exercise

Assessment Version

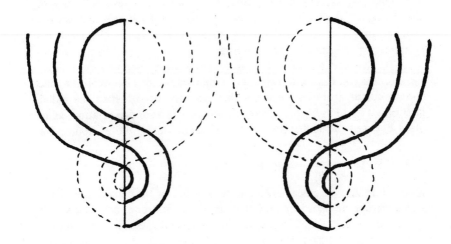

Note: Teacher ——— *; Pupil* - - - - -

Variation for Homework

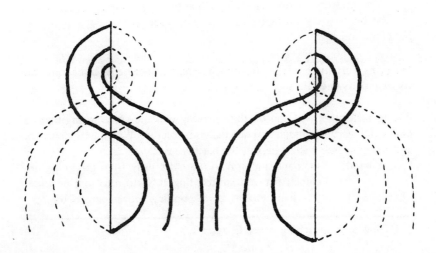

with red corresponding to the right eye on the right of the paper. Other children reverse the colours. We find that when the pupil with the 'reversed' colours has worked for a time at the exercises described in this book his progress is shown by the correct placing of these colours.

One may say that when the eye colour affinity is 'reversed' then the will forces of the individual are held in the habit patterns and organic activities of the body: that he is 'asleep' and lives passively in what he has imitated and inherited from his parents.

To characterise: with this assessment we ask 'Are you riding your horse or are you having to carry it?'. When we succeed in establishing the correct colour affinities we know that we have strengthened the individuality within himself, that there is a full inhalation and exhalation taking place between the soul/spirit and the life body during the 24-hour cycle.

Comment

If the child asks whether he should make a full or half moon, tell him to make the one he likes best. See that there is a full range of colours from which he can choose. Notice with which hand he chooses. Some children will not 'hear', "Draw a blue moon and a red sun", and take yellow instead of red. Others will take a flame red. Some may colour the red over with yellow. Some may surround the red with orange and yellow.

These are all signs of tensions and over-stimulation of the 'stretching' element. As relaxation and harmony are achieved, these extra colours disappear and the carmine red is used.

The crescent moons also 'wax' when the Right-angle Triangle Exercise has been used showing that a balance between 'stretching' and 'lifting' has come about*.

Mirroring Test and Exercise (to show if independence between hearing and visual activity is established: from age 9)

Facing each other, say and do this exercise with the child, seeing that he obeys the *word command* and not the visual picture. With hands clenched, and arms crossed at chest height, the teacher says:

"Right hand" — lift hand and arm to the right away from the body; unclench fist and stretch fingers. Return to first position.
"Left hand" — this hand makes corresponding movement to the left.

---

* 'Lifting' and 'stretching' — see Chapter 1.

"Both and Both Together" — on the word "Both", arms uncross and hands
open. Come to the first position on the word "and".
Repeat the sequence on "Both Together".

Repeat until a good rhythm is established, but make no corrections during the exercise. Let the movement activity penetrate the consciousness: he will 'hear' when the 'lifting' movements are released from the domination of the 'stretching' ones.

Now use the foot. Standing, feet together, the teacher says:

"Right foot" — right foot steps to right side and back to position;
"Left foot"   — left foot to left side, and back to position;
"Jump"   — jump feet astride;
"Cross"   — jump feet crossed over;
"Jump"   — jump feet astride;
"Together"   — jump feet *together.*
Repeat.

When hands and feet no longer mirror the teacher's movements, combine these. Occasionally change the arm movements: up; down; then alternately. If the hand movements are weak and the child unconscious of left-right, let him draw round each hand with a coloured pencil, filling these in. This is a good homework exercise.

Observations

The hands will be flabby with no consciousness in their movement. Generally the upper arms will be held close to the body and a mechanical crossing and uncrossing result. Exaggerate your own arm movements until they are copied.

Overall Body Control (from 7 years)

Let the child lie on the floor and, holding both feet together, raise them as high as possible *without bending the legs.*

Observations

Some children cannot do this, showing there is a gap in the control between 'above-below'. Other children need to lift one leg first before the other can join it. Here the discrepancy between left-right or right-left control shows itself. Start the Crawling Exercises at once with such children.

17

Positional Responses (primitive reflexes: from 7 years)

These are movements where one part of the body causes a specific response in another part. For example, the baby turns his head, the arm on the face side straightens and the arm on the skull side bends. *These responses are normal in the early months of a child's life,* but in some children they are not discarded in the usual course of development and so form 'blockages' to the intended movements which the child wants to make.

We can find out if some of these positional responses are still present by asking the child to place himself in the following positions. Ask the child to lie on his tummy on the floor. Stretch out his arm at the shoulder level make his hands into fists and put them on his shoulders. Then, counting slowly out loud, he is to raise his chest and legs off the floor as high as he can without either his chest collapsing or his legs bending at the knee. If he can hold this position for about 30 seconds, all is well (Landau Reflex).

Now put the child on his hands and knees, arms held straight, and ask him to drop his head between his arms. If the Asymmetric Tonic Neck Reflex remains, then the arms will bend at the elbows, and hips and knees push out as though to straighten. If the head is lifted backwards the arms then straighten, and the child has to follow the movement and sit on his heels. This is evident from birth, and all parents have seen this normal response in their babies. Children with this retained reflex are often the 'non-crawlers'. They are the ones who later cannot see their work properly, neither can they copy from the blackboard as the changing position of the head forces the arms to make responses that hinder their seeing and writing movements.

Retained early patterns of movement are often responsible for delayed movement development. They can be changed. If such movement patterns persist after a period of remedial exercises, the teacher should request that the child see a paediatrician, or that he be referred by his general practitioner to an occupational therapist for further assessment.

Corrective exercises: Creeping and Crawling (page 30), Ball Twirling, adding — for older children — the Copper Ball Exercise.

Ball Throwing (to see if sidedness is properly established and if the above-mentioned positional response has been discarded: from 7 years)

Demonstrate as well as tell: "Throw a ball under the right leg and catch with the other hand. Now throw the ball under the left leg and catch with the right hand. Establish a rhythm. Is he clumsy? Can he lift the leg high enough to throw the ball under it, or does he make a conscious effort? After a time, does he 'cross-over throw', that is, right hand throwing under left leg and vice versa? If this happens, then the soul/spirit is impinging too strongly into the life/physical organisation — weakening the life body. (Look at the Eye-Colour Affinity picture for correlation — see page 22).

Ball Throwing (to see if ambidexterity is overcome: from 7 years)

Demonstrate as well as tell: "Have a soft ball in each hand. Throw one up and pass the other ball into the empty hand. Continue and then reverse". Watch his eyes. Do they follow the ball or stare ahead? When throwing up the ball with the left hand first, often both arms move together — a sign that dominance is not fully established. Both these assessment exercises are also the therapy for the condition they reveal.

Eye Movement (to check that the child's eye can move in all directions freely: from 7 years)

Ask him to look at your finger or a pencil. Hold it fairly near his face and make a clockwise and then anti-clockwise circle, slowly and evenly; then a diagonal movement from right to left and left to right. Pauses or blinking in the smooth rotation of the eye show that there are muscular imbalances. Such things affect the mirror process in reading and eye-hand co-ordination in writing.
Corrective exercises: for younger children, the Rod-rolling Exercise; for older children, the Copper Ball Exercise; for all children the Flower-Rod Exercise will be of importance and the painting exercises will also be necessary.

The Picture of Man-House-Tree (and anything else he wishes to add: from 7 years)

This gives us an overall picture of the child's body geography, spatial orientation and sidedness development. The house is the archetype made up from the square and the triangle — the body and the soul. The details of his house, its windows, chimneys, smoke and door path, show the body geography that the soul has built up in the first seven years. The man gives us an idea of the content which has streamed from the formative forces of the soul into the building of the body. A well-defined figure (head, upper trunk and limbs — the three-fold body — show a harmonious growth

19

of soul powers within the body which should now — after the change of teeth — be free for learning activities. The tree has several connotations: that of the breathing system generally; the nerve element within this; and (the tree with apples) the richness of gifts the soul may be bringing into its life.

If we look at the completed picture, we can see if the spatial orientation is satisfactory. Is the house on the ground? Does the man stand on one side, the tree on the other? Is there a sky and ground (above-below)? Is there a path leading to the house? Has the door a handle (denoting a way in)? Is there a chimney; does smoke come from it (denoting activity in the house)? By observing children and their pictures one learns to 'read' them. (See examples on pages 74 — 80).

To precede this, so that we do not get an 'imaginative' picture but an imprint of the child's relationship to his body, we ask him to do the following: jump as high as he can three or four times; then begin this sequence, standing: 1 — clap alternately in front of and behind the back, counting up to 10; 2 — clap alternately above the head and behind the back, counting up to 10; 3 — clap alternately above the head and in front of the body, counting up to 10; 4 — clap above the head, behind the back, then in front of the body, counting up to 12. Then repeat the four steps of the sequence whilst clapping and jumping.

The resultant picture arises out of the organism in the same way that the eye produces the complementary colours. We see the child's inner objective relationship to his bodily-spatial-movement organisation.

The following assessments are also their own therapy: Hand, Eye, Speech Co-ordination, page 12; Flower-Rod Exercise, page 14; Mirroring Exercise, page 16; Ball Throwing Exercise, pages 18 and 19.

Assessment for School Entry in Class 1 (and for children of Classes 1 — 4)

Place a sheet of plain A4 paper, greatest width left — right, in front of the child. Ask him to draw a line across the paper from left to right. Underneath it, ask him to draw a line in the opposite direction. From this we see if there is a healthy movement relationship between soul and life physical bodies. [Children who break the line and go over it show that the will forces are not at its command. Heavy and too-light pressures show problems of the movement co-ordination]. Now ask the child to draw a wavy line across the page and back to show if the hand is skilled and can alternate between the 'stretching' and 'lifting' elements of the hand. [Children who make the line straight, for example, cannot experience the response of the 'lifting' to the 'stretching' elements. Woolwinding, Marbles between the Toes, Ball Twirling, Hand Stretching Exercises are there to help this condition].

Now draw the empty form of the four-petalled flower and ask the child what it is. If the concept sense and inner visualization is undamaged, then the child will say "a flower". Ask him to complete it and we gain an idea of the activity and health of these aspects.

Continue the assessment with the following: Ball Throwing; Hand, Eye, Speech Co-ordination; Dominance; Handedness Patterns; Eye Movement. Instead of the Flower Rod Exercise, ask the child to draw a lemniscate. Place two dots — one above the other — and yourself draw a figure of 8 around them. Then place the dots for the child and ask him to do what you have done. Inability to cross the 8 after several attempts indicates that a medical examination is necessary. Continue with Eye Colour Affinity, Primitive Reflexes, Overall Body Control, Man-House-Tree Picture. (Children at the end of Class 2 and onwards should be asked to do the Flower-Rod Exercise *and* the Mirroring Exercise).

Levels of Diagnosis

The assessments show us what we already suspect on one or another level. They confirm that our observations are right. Therefore they act as a warning: "Watch and see where the trouble is going to show itself and take action before the situation has become a fixed one".

The Eye-Colour Affinity assessment tells us *to look*. . .

— At the child's constitution. Is it sickly? Has he poor breathing? Does he have constant minor ailments?

If the nerve sense system is in good order, then writing and reading need not be affected. If the child's vitality has suffered then it is more likely that the nerve sense system has been over-stimulated.

— At behaviour problems in classroom and at home. Is environment and heredity making him 'carry the horse'?

— At intellectual faculty development.

A blockage of one of the above levels is likely to occur unless help is given.

If the Flower-Rod drawing is also poor, then the trouble has gone deep and results will take longer to appear.

If there is an aberration in the Cross assessment — see page 10 —

where the child draws a line across the vertical one dividing the page, development will be very slow and difficult and, with certain types of case histories, we may suspect physiological damage.

The following classroom observations tell us that our pupil needs an assessment to find out the particular needs of his problem:

a child who writes with his head on his arm;

a child who constantly looks at the board when writing;

a child who fidgets and disturbs the class continually;

a child who stands helplessly in the playground and lets children bump into him;

a clumsy child who stumbles and drops things;

a child who runs about wildly, crashing into other children, and who never plays with them;

a child who prefers playing with much younger children;

a child who cannot catch a ball easily;

a child who stumbles in his speech, omitting or adding extra syllables to words;

a child who cannot form his sentences, cannot find the words he needs;

a child who cannot write neatly and cannot hold his pencil comfortably.

All these are symptoms of co-ordination/spatial orientation problems and incomplete development of stages between one and seven years, and need immediate attention before the secondary psychological reactions set in.

The simplest diagnostic observation that we can make is to notice which children in the class choose their crayon or pencil with the left hand and then pass it to their right hand for use. These children are already in difficulty with their body geography and spatial orientation. They, like the others already mentioned, need immediate help so that development of faculty can proceed normally.

Important note on the independence between Sight, Dominance and Eye-Colour Affinity: they in no way condition each other. Strength of sight, long or short sight, one eye stronger than the other, astigmatism — these belong to the physical constitution and do not affect dominance choice, e.g. a child can have a strong-sighted left eye with well established right-eyed and right-handed dominance.

Eye-Colour Affinity (inner relationship to space — see pages 14, 16, 80, and 81)

Eye-Colour Affinity — blue for left eye, red for right eye — is usually established between the ages of 6 — 7 years. This, with the Cross test

22

(see page 10), are the only two assessment factors which are not in themselves a therapy exercise which can be used in the lessons. The Eye-Colour Affinity assessment can become a living language for the teacher; it is an answer which the child gives to the unspoken question: "Are you able to get into your body, are you properly 'awake' in it yourself?".

It should be noted that Eye-Colour Affinity is in no way related to dominance or sidedness. A child with fully-established left-hand dominance can have correct Eye-Colour Affinity, as can children with poor sight in one or both eyes. When the colours are 'reversed' (red on the left, blue on the right) in a child with apparently no problems, it shows that he is in the process of adapting to a new stage of development and the 'reversal' corrects itself when this step is completed — for example, during the ninth year, when the child feels himself as a separate entity from his environment*. It can 'reverse' when the child is over-strained physically or intellectually or when there are emotional difficulties in the home life, e.g. difficulties between parents or, for a time, before and after illness. 'Reversals' are a means of an early warning of trouble which could be resolved by using a suitable exercise from one of the given groups. When it corrects itself it shows that the child is strong enough to continue his development unaided.

Experience has shown that if unusual aberration of colour choice is repeated, i.e. red-yellow, or mixing colours on top of each other, together with unnatural placing of the forms — i.e. at extreme corners of the paper, or very close together — it means that the child should be seen by a psychiatric doctor. The problems for which he has been sent to us are stemming from deeper causes than those which can be helped by educational means alone.

When giving the Eye-Colour Affinity assessment, the phraseology used and order of the colours have been given *in all possible variations*, but in general practice it is advisable to keep to its natural sequence as in writing, i.e. from left to right: moon-sun. This assessment has been given by colleagues to classes as a whole. It has also been given individually to all children in a class. (See Interpretation section, pages 74 – 80).

Dominance

Preference for use of one side of the body; for the majority of people the right side.

---

*See König *The First Three Years of the Child*, page 121

23

Further Remarks

Continuing research is bringing to our attention that there are children who lack spatial orientation and body geography, yet have no overt learning problems. The absence of these important stages is a hindrance to future cognitive capacities in relation to self-recognition and finding one's place in the world. These children also need our attention, and they can acquire these basic faculties after a period of the necessary relevant exercises.

The reasons for such a condition are manifold, for example: the constant demand for earlier and earlier attainment of the stages of development in the first years; helping the child to walk before he is ready; giving him a tricycle or pedal-car before he is firmly on his feet. Constant car transport, insufficient walking in distances, long periods of watching T.V. instead of creative play, the immediate availability of videos and computers — these are all robbing the child of his play-time and the experience of using his body. The pressure on children to 'learn' has silenced the question: "What are the appropriate experiences a child should have at a particular stage of his growth and development?".

Chapter Four

THE EXERCISES

These exercises have been done with children from 11 to 14 years of age and over. The pupil has come to the teacher's home once a week for an hour, the younger ones during school time, the older ones at 4 p.m.

Some children who were unable to respond to a weekly rhythm have come daily for two weeks for the main work, continuing to come each morning for ten minutes before school for one specific exercise.

Another successful time sequence is to take a child daily out of lessons for twenty minutes over a period of eight weeks. This is practicable when the work is done in the school.

In the course of the last 10 years, problems have become apparent in younger and younger children. It appears vital now to assess children at the age of 8-plus, as many of the problems are already showing themselves by then; much misery and frustration can be avoided by prompt action.

All exercises can be used from the age of 11 years. Prior to that, the age from which a particular exercise may be used will be indicated.

Body Geography (from 11 years)

The pupil stands in front of the teacher who gives the following directions:

1st type: Touch your head with your right hand.
Touch your left knee with your nose, etc.

2nd type: Place your right hand on your left shoulder.
Your left hand on your head : change : change.
Place your left hand on your chin, right hand on your right knee: change: change.
Hold your left ear with left hand.
Ditto right ear with right hand.
Cross over: left ear : right hand)
           right ear : left hand) in one movement.
Right hand on your nose.
Left hand on right ear. Change.
Reverse this, etc. and continue using as many combinations as possible.

3rd type: Ear-Eye independence.
Use the Mirroring Exercise described in Assessment section.

For Classes 1 – 3 and individual children 7 – 10 years

As dominance is no longer educated through children's games, and parental guidance in using the right side of the body for practical activities (opening a door, putting first the right arm into the coat sleeve, etc.), we need to help the children to establish their dominance. A surprising number of children are uncertain which is their right hand or left hand. Among other factors, our use of the term "That's right" for the meaning of "That's correct" can be a cause of confusion. It is better for younger children to name the right side of the body and use the term "Other hand", etc., for the left side.

The teacher gives instruction. He does *not* do the movements, otherwise the child is likely to mirror them instead of reversing them. The teacher could use the following references:

Class 1 (7th year – 8)

Use right hand and limb only to touch different parts of the body.

Class 2 (8 plus)

Use right hand to touch right side of the body; the 'other' hand to touch the other side.

Class 3 (8 – 11 years)

Use the right hand to touch the left side of the body; use the 'left' hand (introducing the term) to touch the right side of the body. This correlates with the change of consciousness in the ninth year.

Wool Winding and Skein Twisting (from 7 years)

Using a ball of blue wool, let the pupil wind it between the little finger and thumb of the left hand in a figure of eight.

The hand must *remain fully stretched* and the wool wound clockwise *over* the little finger, then *under* it, and over the thumb anti-clockwise.

Repeat with red wool on right hand, winding directions reversed.

Observations

This exercise brings into play the movement between the radius and ulna bones of the lower arm – the changing from 'stretching' to 'lifting' man. Winding the wool in the given directions brings about maximum turning movement. The wool will become drawn tighter and tighter until thumb and little finger are bound together. The child should stand with his feet parallel but a little apart. Watch how the movement calls on the whole

26

body and how it is obstructed in its flow — weight goes on one leg, hip twists, shoulder humps, etc. Relaxed skilful winding should be achieved (use nearly half a ball of wool). When rewinding the wool on to the ball, see that it is wound 'clockwise' from the body to 'in front'. Children will wind it towards themselves which is a contra-movement to the natural arm movement.

Skein Twisting (from 7 years)

A skein of wool is a new phenomenon to the modern child: make one on his arms from a ball of wool. Tie in three places. He should now twist it until it is tight by turning his right wrist, then untwist until it is tight again. Untwist until slack. Repeat with left wrist. Now both arms together. When he is able to do this skilfully with the wool on his arms, change to holding it on his hands between the socket of his thumb and first finger. Always end with the skein twisted into the beautiful figure of 8, its ends interlocked.

Observations

Much popping of muscles under the shoulder blade areas in early attempts and confusion of directions in arm twisting movements. Note the phenomenon of how twisting continuously in the same direction finally makes the movement in the skein reverse back on itself.

This is the motif behind the over-stimulation of the senses of the 'stretching man'. To protect himself from excessive sense impressions, the movement is reversed so blocking the natural response of the 'lifting man', i.e. the astral (soul) body cannot release itself from the life/physical bodies and the synapse becomes 'blocked'.

Marbles (from 7 years)

Having activated 'lifting' movements in the upper part of the body, we will. now try to do something down below.

Let the pupil remove his socks after asking if his feet are clean or would he prefer to do it next time. He should then tuck a marble between the big toes of each foot and wriggle them out easily. Then the next pair of toes and so on to the little toes — long pause and much wriggling. See that the marbles are placed fully into the toe sockets! Note: some children's feet are so flabby they cannot hold the marbles so change to picking them up with toes and dropping them. Also walking with marbles tucked between toes.

27

Many immobile unconscious feet present themselves to the gaze. The movement from the feet runs right into the fingers and backs of the hands and up into the jaw — emphasis usually on one or other side — make a note of this as it will help to decide movement sequence in the painting exercises which will be given later. This is a most popular exercise with all ages; 15- and 16-year olds are nonplussed at their own inability. The reactions are most informative about their characters.

Spatial Orientation Exercises

To Bring Awareness of Left and Right (from 7 years)

Required: two soft felt balls, preferably in blue and red. Woolly balls are also suitable. The pupil has one in each hand. He is told to throw up the one in his right hand; as he does so he has to pass the ball held in his left hand into the right hand, catching the returning ball in the left hand. Repeat until a rhythm is established. Now reverse the direction starting with the left hand.

Observations

The exercise makes the child aware of left/right in 'lifting' movements. Often both balls are thrown up together showing that his will does not penetrate the body. He may be skilled with throwing the ball up with his right hand first, but when reversing the sequence the right hand follows the left hand movement, showing the right side is not independent of the activity of the left side; thus his individual will is not in command of the bodily situation. The opposite may also occur — left dominated by right.

We can also see how dependent some children have become on the stretching movements. They 'overbalance' into them, snatching the ball out of the air with a downward grab of the hand. *This need to clutch hold of sense impressions* can be rectified by the Ball Twirling and Bouncing Exercises.

Having called on consciousness in left and right-sidedness, we will now bring this into relationship with *Above to Below.*

With a ball in each hand throw the ball in the right hand under the right leg from outside and catch it with the same hand. Repeat on left side. When rhythm is established, walk forward and back saying the Alphabet forward and then backwards.

Observations

Difficulty in making effort to lift legs high enough, particularly left leg. Crossing over the movement, i.e. throwing right hand ball under left leg, left hand ball under right leg, showing he is unable to maintain independence throughout whole body area (note relationship of these movements to convex-concave mirror process — Chapter 2). Practise until skill in movement and co-ordination of movement, speaking and thinking is accomplished.

Variation of this exercise: let the child sit and clap hands under one leg, then clap above and clap under the other leg, then above, counting to 100 and back or saying multiplication tables forward and back.

To Bring Awareness of Forward and Backward (from 7 years)

Required: a copper rod, i.e. ½" plumber's copper piping, ends filed smooth or fitted with rubber caps — temporarily a walking stick can be used.

Grasp the rod vertically right hand above left and hold out at arm's length. Walk forward and back, counting aloud or saying a chosen sentence, stepping on each number or word: minimum 3 times. Change the position of the rod to behind the back, holding it against the spine. Repeat walking-speaking combination. For very bad posture — round shoulders, slovenly sitting positions — hold the rod horizontally across the shoulders and walk, etc.

Observations

Note which direction gives difficulty. Is there quick or slow improvement? If slow, this can be supported and improved by the painting exercises.

Exercise with Whole Body (from 9 years)

Stand feet together, fists clenched. Lift arms forward and make pulling, pummelling movement, so that shoulders are pulled on each side of neck. Continue: pummelling the ceiling;

pummelling walls on left and right side (arms held horizontally);

bent forward, head hanging loosely, pummelling the floor.

Note stiffness on either of the sides of the body and possible crick in the neck when bent forwards: to correct this try Triangle-Rod Exercise (see page 34). This pummelling exercise is a popular one with forceful, frustrated children.

To Integrate the Positional Responses — Primitive Reflexes (from 6 years)

Practice Creeping and Crawling with the children (as described on pages 3 and 18).

Creeping: Left — Right — Horizontal (from 7 years)

In spite of many children being agile in climbing, running and gym, these exercises revealed underground tensions in the subtler movements, so every way of bringing activity into unused parts of the body was explored.

Getting the children to 'creep' with *forearms* on the ground revealed many a hidden gesture that was being held unconsciously within the body. Some children 'crept' with their chins cupped in the hands, having raised the arms on to their elbows. Others clenched their fists until the knuckles were white and 'crept' arm over arm with the hand held towards the body as though they were gathering everything to their chests. Sometimes one leg lagged behind or could not bend, or feet were lifeless and dragged along. All children experienced the dragging weight of the body and often their necks were locked between the shoulder blades so that turning was difficult. To help this the children were shown the 'Caterpillar Crawl'.

Caterpillar Crawl: Above — Below — Horizontal (from 7 years)

Lying on the back push with the heels until body moves backwards along the floor the length of the room, reverse direction by pulling on the heels. No help from the arms is allowed.

The Grand Crawl (from 7 years)

Kneel on the floor, stretch right arm back as far as it will go, bring it over the head (at the side) and place palm on the floor in front as far as the arm can stretch. Now bring the right knee up to the hand. The eyes and head should follow the hand movement all the time. Repeat with left hand and leg, and continue along the floor in a steady rhythm.

The Wrestle: Boys Only (from 11 years)

Lying face downwards arms behind the back, left hand holding right elbow, right hand holding left elbow, wriggle the length of the room without letting go of the elbows. If arms are released the 'opponent' wins.

Exercises for Developing Sense of Rhythm
with Harmonization of Body Space and Breathing

The Copper Ball Exercise* (from 10 years)

Required: two copper balls or two medium-sized oranges and a soft ball. If available, this exercise can be accompanied by the teacher playing a scale up and down on a Choroi lyre or pentatonic Kalimba.

Let the child lie flat on his back, arms at his sides with the palms uppermost, holding the balls. Place the soft ball between big toe joints so that feet are kept together.

Part 1: Lift head until one of the hands can be seen (free choice). Gazing at the ball, lift the arm slowly into the vertical position. At the moment the ball would fall, turn the hand and continue the movement backwards until arm reaches the floor, turning the head and following the movement through *with the eyes* until the arm is fully extended and then relaxed on to the floor.

Repeat with the other arm.

Turn gaze to the first arm which was used. Bring it back to the side of the body, reversing hand direction at midway position. Relax.

Repeat with the other arm.

Continue this rhythm, always emphasizing the relaxation between movements so that child lets go the tension in the stretching movement and has to find the unaccustomed, unused areas of the lifting movement. Gradually increase the time to 5 – 7 minutes.

Part 2: With eyes closed and both hands at sides lift them together, turning

---

* Note Steiner's description of the centres for visual and auditory memory in *Meditatively Acquired Knowledge of Man* – lecture 4, 22.9.1920, "The Art of Education Consists of Bringing into Balance the Physical and Spiritual Nature of the Developing Human Being".

them when they are vertical to the floor and thoroughly relaxing the movement when they are resting on the floor at back of the head. Return as before and repeat. Increase time gradually to 5 – 7 minutes.

Part 3: Eyes still closed, one hand above head, other on floor (free choice). Move hands at the same time until positions are reversed, sensing the 'turning' movement required when arms are level with each other. Time 5 – 7 minutes.

When accompanying this exercise with music *keep in time with the child's movements;* do not impose your will and rhythm on his.

Observations

This is one of the most important exercises and eloquently reveals the child's situation. The dominant hand may not be the one chosen with which to start. The feet will fall apart: replace the ball for him. On the downward movement the hand may not turn in the right direction – should this difficulty persist after about 6 – 8 lessons, wrap a 1 lb. bag of sugar in a cloth, let the child lift it with his hand from the 'wrong' outward position into the right one. Repeat several times.

The turning may begin to be slurred, only taking place just before arm reaches the floor. Arms may not relax fully – they can be bent and drawn down until the shoulders lie flat on the floor. This relaxation pause between movements is the most important part of the exercise.

Eyes – when open child will forget to follow the movement and gaze straight ahead. He may have to look down before being able to look up.

When the eyes are closed, twitching, squinting and flickering movements will be present, sometimes the balls of the eyes rolling towards the arms as though dragged by the movement. Jaw movements from side to side will start as the exercise penetrates the body.

When the arms are moving alternately one arm may have to stop and go backwards before the arm opposite can complete its movement.

At a certain point children suddenly become unrhythmical, scarcely pausing between movements; this is the symptom of a definite stage and has to be gone through. Some children hold their breath against the movement. These are all results of the rush and hurry and pressures to which they have succumbed. Children who are very tense and living too strongly in the stretching movements will find when they really relax that at first they cannot get up at the end of the exercise – this shows us what a small area of the body they are capable of using. Note how the quality of the movement changes from quick, slick lifting, to a conscious carrying and placing.

Some children will have to lift head and shoulders from the floor in order to follow the movement from below to above. The eyes may close as the head turns from one side to the other – use Pummelling Exercise and Rod-rolling Exercise to release this. Watch the lips: often one or more of the vowel sounds are formed by them as the movements reach deeper into the body.

Good signs

When all the mentioned movements stop and the child begins to move harmoniously; when big breaths are taken; when sighing and yawning begin; when a peaceful atmosphere envelopes child and teacher.

Always follow this exercise by the Moving Straight Line and Lemniscate Exercise to be described later.

Ball Twirling Exercise: Introduction for 3-fold Spiral (from 8 years)

Stand with a copper ball or orange in each hand and a copper ball or tennis ball under one foot. Lift one hand and turn the ball by moving the thumb from direction of the little finger across the hand (anti-clockwise for right hand). When the movement is established, raise the other hand, always moving the ball by taking the thumb from the little finger across the palm of the hand.

Add the foot movement by rolling the ball inwards round and round, controlling the ball with the sole of the foot. Now say a Rhyme – a nursery rhyme or jingle is suitable. Keep everything moving! Repeat with the other foot.

Observations

Notice to which hand the eye clings, which leg reverses its direction, which hand or hands forget to move.

The child should become skilful enough to hold the arms well up and gaze ahead with confidence.

In these exercises the obstruction to the flow of movement causing the dominance changes becomes visible.

The Three-fold Spiral (from 6 years)

This is a good exercise for restless fidgety children; those who dream or who have any sleeping difficulties.

33

Draw a large RIGHT HAND clockwise spiral to centre on a large sheet
of strong paper or card, 20" x 30"
(55 cm x 75 cm); place it flat on
the floor.

The child sits on a comfortably low chair in front of the paper, holding a copper ball or an object — crystal — in the left hand. The right foot
starts in the centre of the spiral and moves to the outside, the left foot
then takes over the ending position of the right foot and moves to the
centre. At the centre remove the foot. Sitting with his feet together, the
child leans forward and, with his *right* hand, draws the spiral from the
outside to the centre. Repeat these three movements 12 times, increasing
the exercise time to 15 minutes.

The choice of the starting foot is free, but the movements of both
feet are 'inwards'. Always use the right hand. The left hand remains still,
holding the copper ball or weighted object. This applies to *both right- and
left-handed children.*

Observations

Sudden errors and repetition of the same foot; the hand starting at the
inside of the spiral.

This and the Twirling Exercise are the only two which one corrects
as they are done. Just make a suitable sound!

Triangle-Rod Exercise and Verse* (from 12 years)

The copper rod is placed on the floor in front of the feet. The child stands
with palms of hands held together, fingers to wrists horizontal to the floor.

The teacher says: "Weight presses downwards".

The pupil lifts and places first left, and then right foot astride, the
width of the rod.

The teacher says: "Light streams upwards".

Hands and arms are lifted from centre outwards and up, the distance
between them matching the width of the feet and rod.

Keeping the hands the same distance apart he bends forward, head
between arms until he touches the rod. Lift the rod, carry it upward until
the arms are over the head. Slowly return the rod to the floor — head and

---

*After an exercise given by Rudolf Steiner, 12.1.1924.

34

arms level, please! Raise the arms and body back to original position. Jump, feet together, arms to sides. Repeat three times.

Observations

The child's comments proclaim the necessity for this exercise.

There is always difficulty with the position of the head between the arms. The head pokes forwards; the neck is caught in a 'crick'; the knees are too stiff and the child has to crouch in order to put the rod on to the floor. When accomplished, great satisfaction for both pupil and teacher!

Establishing Dominance
on the Right or Left Side of the Body

For children between 6 − 11 years of age use this exercise. Make a large drawing on a sheet of light card, copying the drawing below. Place it upright against the wall. The child sits on the floor in front of it and draws it with the same sequence of body movements as given for the Right-angle Triangle Exercise (see below). If this child is to remain left handed on the school doctor's advice, the sequence should be: both feet; left foot; left foot and left eye; left foot and left hand, etc.

Right-angle Triangle Exercise (from 11 years)

On two large cards 30" x 20" (75 cm x 55cm) draw triangles, one on each side, coloured and numbered as illustrations on pages 36 and 37, using the whole area of the cards.

This is the exercise to improve and bring the corrections shown to be necessary from the Handedness Assessment.

The child sits in front of card A, which is placed upright against the wall.

Part 1: Using both feet held together. . .

Draw from the number to the arrow. Place the feet back on to the floor between each number. Repeat three times.

Part 2: Now draw the triangle with. . .

Right foot. Repeat three times.

35

Right-Angle Triangle Exercise

For a Right-handed Child

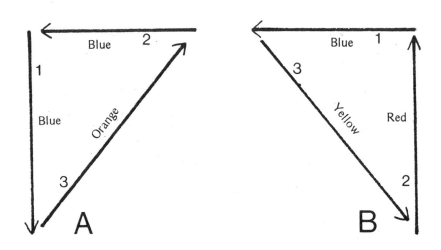

Note: Draw each triangle, A, B, C, D, on a separate card

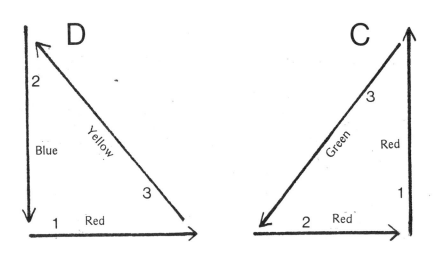

Right-Angle Triangle Exercise

For a Left-handed Child

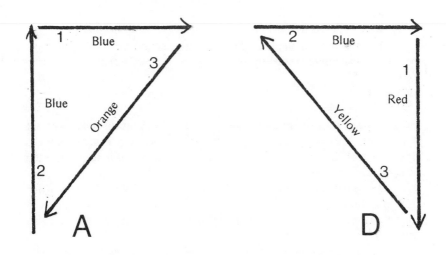

Note: Draw each triangle A, B, C, D, on a separate card

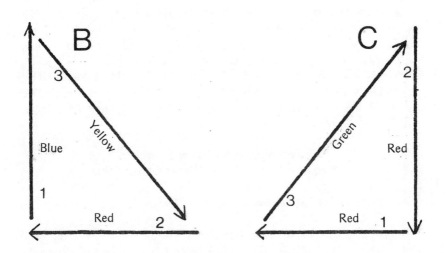

Right foot, right eye. Repeat movement as before.

Right foot, right hand, right eye.

Both hands held together. Place both hands back into lap between each movement.

Right hand. . . Right hand, right eye.

Right eye (cover left eye with hand).

With the nose (teacher chooses a part of the body at random).

Repeat with each Triangle. (Whole exercise takes 12 minutes). Variation: each limb movement once only (5 – 7 minutes).

Observations

This shows us the poor body geography, the memory blocks and movement hesitations. This exercise confirms dominance; it also enlivens and increases the power of the child to overcome the instinct impulses imitated into the organism in the first seven years.

We see this in the change to the correct Eye-Colour Affinity when retested. Children who have made a crescent-moon shape in this test will often change to a 'full' moon, telling us there is an increase of liveliness in the left side of the body.

As experience grows the teacher will sometimes detect that immobility of the non-dominant side of the body is causing obstruction to progress. A guide to this is the careful observation of the eyes. One of them is more fixed in expression or direction of gaze: this can also be confirmed from the Handedness Pattern by the sudden change of eye in one of the sequences. We should now give the right-handed child the triangle sequence for the left side of the body for a short period of time, e.g. daily for 2 – 3 weeks, or at least six times if the lesson is weekly. Similarly the left-handed child should do the right side sequence. This exercise is based on the correct movement pattern for the respective sides of the body and therefore does not induce ambidexterity. Check result with Eye Colour Affinity assessment.

Stretching and Lifting Exercises
in Relation to the Three Dimensions of Space

Weight-lifting Exercise: Above-Below (from 7 years)

Pupil and teacher stand facing each other. Ask the child how heavy he is. Help him to realize that the human being has the wonderful capacity to carry such weight effortlessly. We will now experience the weight and how we can lift it.

Let him imagine a straight line drawn from a star over his head through him to the centre of the earth. With eyes gazing straight ahead at a chosen spot he is to lift his toes as high as they will go without the soles of his feet lifting from the floor. Now lower the toes and press them hard against the floor gripping it as strongly as possible. Repeat twice more and then, raising the heels, stand on the toes, the ball of the foot off the floor: very slowly lower the heels to standing position. Repeat whole exercise twice more. See that the hands remain at the sides of the body. In standing before an adult many children clasp their hands behind their backs.

Observations

Stiff feet: one foot more so than the other — which?. Both feet rolling over onto little toes and ankles.

After the second time the hands begin tensing, backs of the hands may be drawn back: the first fingers of one or both hands stiffen and point or the little fingers of one or both hands stiffen and are pulled sideways from the rest of the hand.

When the first fingers are separated out from the hand, then the child has had intellectual demands made too early in his development; he has managed to meet them at the expense of his capacity to meet behaviour and concentration demands. The whole hand pulled backwards shows that the child has been under great pressure.

If the little fingers are pulled away from the hand, then the child is having difficulty to meet intellectual and behaviour requirements and is sinking back into imitation of habits, etc., in his environment. The exercise helps to release tensions and to strengthen the experience of the 'lifting' element in which his own will forces are working. 'Two finger' knitting is an excellent corrective.

Bouncing Balls: Left-Right (from 8 years)

Required: two of the large football-sized bouncing balls, blue and red if available.

Holding a ball on the palm of each hand, bounce the ball in one hand and catch it on the palm of the same hand. Repeat with the other hand. Alternating the hands, count forward to a given number and back. Give plenty of practice to unused number sequences, e.g. 863 — 1039.

This brings great flexibility between the stretching and lifting element. It requires will forces and concentration. Especially good for lazy, slow thinkers and bad memories, also for children who are reluctant to move themselves. Extend the child's physical capacity as far as possible. It is not too much for a 13- or 14-year old to count to 1000.

Rod Rolling: Forward and Back (from 7 years)

Required: a copper rod.

Pupil and teacher must face each other, arms held forwards, palms uppermost, rod across the hands of the teacher who rolls it back over his arms to touch his throat. It is then rolled back on to the outstretched hands of the pupil, who copies this movement. As he does this, the teacher mirrors the arm movements up and down, then receives the rod again. The pupil copies this as the rod rolls on the teacher's arms. Continue rhythmically, Singing helps (Skye Boat Song).

Observations

This soon brings out the weakness of the upper arms and the hidden gestures making the constriction which holds them tucked into the sides. Often the arms turn over hands downward into the stretching gesture when the rod rolls down. Sometimes the tension is so strong that the hands can only be turned upward again by swinging the whole arm backwards, then round and forward. Shallow breathing is exposed and corrected by this exercise.

Note how the eyes cloud over in this and the Weight Lifting Exercise as the will of the child tries to penetrate the body. As the capacity to penetrate his body grows, so the eyes clear and remain shining.

Drawing Exercises

When the child is writing his name during the assessment we can observe how he handles the pencil. Is it held correctly between first finger and thumb and supported by the third finger? There are some very strange 'grips' on pencils to be seen! Is it held far too tightly, the whole hand rigid, the shoulder humped or held tightly to the body? How are the feet placed?

The elements of good positions for work need to be taught nowadays. (This is essential if children are to enjoy and enter into the movements required in the Eurythmy lessons). Natural grace and feeling for beauty in the movement and the form is fast diminishing. Many educationalists are working to re-establish this.

So, for good writing position, we will start at the feet. See that the whole foot is resting on the floor all the time. The chair should not be so high that the child has to sit tipped forward; he should be sitting with hips slightly lower than the level of the knees so that the arm movements can reach right through the body. Also, the table height needs to be low enough for the arm to rest on it without the shoulder being forced up again, thus arresting the full flow of the arm movement.

The sheet of paper in front of the child brings his consciousness immediately into a two-dimensional relationship between it and him. It should be large and kept perfectly straight. The child must be able to move from a feeling inside himself across and up and down and around the paper. If the paper moves then the child feels himself as a fixed point about which space revolves.

The Body Geography Exercises will help to loosen the hand-arm movements. A way of helping the child to move across the writing area is to practice expansion and contraction movements across the table, first without, and then holding, the pencil. Place the hand over to the left side of the table, fist clenched; maintaining position of the thumb, stretch the hand to its full width; clench the hand to the little finger. From the new position of the thumb, again stretch and contract the hand until the edge of the table is reached. Then repeat the process, holding a pencil.

To release the pressure of the hand when holding the pencil, we can work in two ways: directly, by getting the child to lift the index finger off the pencil; indirectly, to make the hand mobile, by making the foot skilful, i.e. by getting the child to write forms and letters with his foot. (Right for right-handed children; left for left-handed children).

Experience has shown that children are willing and delighted to repeat the earliest drawing movement in their development — the 'scribbled whirl'*. So give the child a large sheet of paper and a wax crayon, and let him make an in-going circular whirl from right to left. Let him do this as a regular prelude to continuous pattern exercises until he relaxes and enjoys this by putting his whole energy into the movement. With the children of 11 years onwards, it should be followed by the

* See Strauss, M. *Understanding Children's Drawings*

continuous clockwise spiral pattern across the paper from left to right.

The first drawing exercises are continuous patterns — teachers may make their own; some examples are illustrated (see Appendix, page 86). The following methods of introducing them are aimed at eye-hand co-ordination, relaxation and rhythm.

"The eye should lovingly follow what the hand does." R. Steiner.

1. Let the child practice the pattern in the air, moving around it with the whole palm of the hand;
2. Take a feather and do the same;
3. Now with the finger;
4. Cover the left eye and repeat with eye and finger;
5. Shut both eyes and make the pattern with the hand;
6. Cover the left eye* and look the pattern through with the right eye;
7. Now close both eyes and look the pattern through. Watch movement of the eyeballs under the closed lids.

Watch carefully that the child does this actively. When drawing, see that the movement of heavy to light both in weight and colour is experienced.

The following exercises should be done (see illustrations):

A. Exercises in Mirroring on vertical and horizontal axis, page 87;
B. The Flower-Rod Exercise — See "Assessment", page 15;
C. Lemniscates in Directions of Space — as illustrated, page 83;
D. Area Exercise — as illustrated, page 87;
E. Interpenetrating Triangle Exercise, page 85)   for children
F. Geometry of the Hexagon   ) from 11 years onwards

Moving Straight Line and Lemniscate Exercise (from 8 years)

For use as an independent exercise, and *always* after the Copper Ball Exercise.

This exercise is done sitting in front of a table or a flat desk placed lengthwise. The chair must be of a height so that in sitting the knees are slightly higher than the hips. The feet, held together, should be firmly

---

* With blue. If changing dominance, see Counting Star Exercise, page 45

Moving Straight Line and Lemniscate

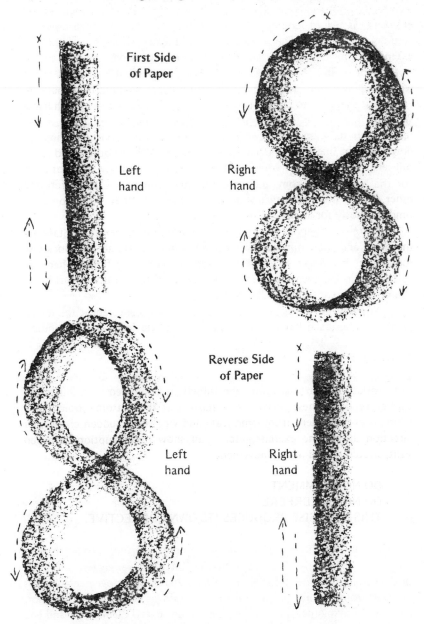

First Side
of Paper

Left
hand

Right
hand

Reverse Side
of Paper

Left
hand

Right
hand

on the floor. The paper, approximately 24" x 15" (55 cm x 38cm) — architect's photo-stats or the backs of posters from travel agencies are excellent, is placed lengthwise in front of the child and fixed down or held by the teacher. The pupil's arms should reach forward to the full extent of the paper, and the form should reach from the top to the bottom of it. In this way a kind of 'rowing' movement is brought about with a full swinging movement passing from the spine up to the shoulders.

Ask the child to choose two colour block crayons, one in each hand. With all fingers firmly held on to the block so that the long side of the rectangle is fully on the paper, he is to draw a continuously moving up-down straight line with one hand and a large '8' with the other hand, both full length of the paper, while the teacher holds it firmly. Choice of form for the hand is left completely free; he may commence one before the other if he wishes when learning the exercises, but they should be done simultaneously for about 3 – 6 minutes.

To relax fingers at the end of the first part of the exercise, stand by the pupil and show him your right hand. Wind the thumb anti-clockwise round the first finger several times. Repeat round each finger. There are suitable four-line poems to use with this movement. Repeat with left hand; thumb movement CLOCKWISE round each finger.

Now reverse the paper: change block crayons and repeat the movement exercise, each hand now having the opposite form; 3 – 6 minutes.

Observations

Note variety of starting points and directions compared with illustrated correct version. These variations — starting at the bottom; straight line taking over movement from lemniscate and vice versa; sudden changes of direction during the exercise, etc. — all show the disruptions between sight, stretching and lifting movements.

DO NOT COMMENT
DO NOT INTERFERE
THIS EXERCISE PRODUCES ITS OWN CORRECTIVE.

Simply watch. If the counter movements are very strong, shorten the time. ONLY IN THE SECOND TERM may we suggest AT THE BEGINNING of the exercise that the child makes the movement towards or away from the line, or just run one's own finger in the correct direction and say: "Follow that way". If he does not do so, NO COMMENT and NO

CORRECTION. Just say the same thing next lesson very softly, very gently and patiently wait, leaving further instruction aside for several lessons. A sensitivity in doing this will develop.

The movement of the arms extends the chest; breathing is deepened; expansion and contraction, forward and back movements come into play; the eyes have to watch the hands; concentration is controlled. See that the feet are firmly on the ground and that the chair is not too high. It is *important* that the child sits well back, spine and hips fully taking up the movement. See that the fingers, *especially little fingers,* are all holding the block.

The Counting Star (from 7 years; see illustration on page 85)

For changing dominance from left eye to right eye in right-handed children. Cover left eye with blue lens inserted into old frame of sunglasses — blue lighting gelatine, double thickness, makes a suitable lens.

This exercise is done standing facing a blackboard or large sheet of paper, 26" x 24" (67 cm x 61cm) or larger according to height of pupil. The feet should be slightly apart, but kept parallel during the exercise. It is important that the pupil does not slouch or have the body weight more on one leg than the other.

The pupil should make the circle with the chosen number of points. At first, if it is cramped, the teacher may put one point at the top of the paper and another at the bottom, and tell the pupil to fill-in the other points. It is important that he makes his own attempt before this is done. Do not suggest a clock-face; let him solve the spacing problem as part of the exercise in finding his own inner space in relation to the two-dimensional surface and movement. The exercise is done as follows:

Make a circle with 12 equally-spaced points. *From* any chosen point, count 5, draw a line from the chosen starting point to the fifth place. From there count another 5 points. Starting *from* the line already drawn, continue it to the new position. The arm should be fully extended and the drawing made with large sweeping movements making the whole body active in expansion and contraction. Repeat, always moving in a *clockwise* direction until the line returns to the starting point. The same clockwise direction is kept even when the pupil is left-handed; that is, the writing direction of left to right is maintained. The star may be coloured in for homework. Any number of points in a circle can be chosen. The lines must intersect, touch each point and return to starting place. The arm must be extended to its full length when drawing from one point to the next, so that a sweeping movement is used.

Observations

See that the right hand moves with the counting — which should be spoken aloud. The left hand should mark the position to which the line is to be drawn. Always move clockwise.

This exercise is also good for slow lethargic thinkers and movers, as well as for the child with quick superficial abilities. A salutary concentration exercise, as well as of interest to the mathematically-minded child.

Here are the number sequences for the circles which, when counted, go to each point and close the circle producing a star.
Example: on a circle of 12 points counting with any of the numbers (5 or 7) will go to each point and make a star (see page 85).

Number of points in circle	Counting numbers
5	2
7	3,4
11	4,5,6,7
12	5,7
13	5,6,7,8
15	4,7,8,11
16	7,9
17	4,7,8,9,10,13
18	5,7,11,13
19	5,6,7,8,10,11,12,13,14
20	7,9,11,13

Triangles (see illustration on page 85)

Interpenetrating Triangles (freehand drawing throughout):
Draw two equilateral triangles, apex to apex. Move the top one into the lower one in a freely chosen number of steps until a 6-pointed star appears. Colour the base triangle in one colour and points of moving triangle in another. Repeat with new pair of triangles, moving the lower one into the upper. Repeat moving each triangle alternately, one step towards the other until the star appears.

Observations

Aim. Exactness through eye-hand co-ordination and judgment.

This exercise gives a real experience of the connection between free choice and responsibility for what has been chosen. It is most salutary for teenage problems. Note enlargement or contraction of triangle, also the timidity in the closeness of the 'steps' which appears.

Geometry of Hexagon (from 12 years)

Cover drawing paper with harmonious interlacing circles (radius six times into circumference to make 'lazy daisy' pattern).

The effective element in this exercise is not so much the resultant geometrical forms, but the constant necessity to repeat the circular pattern.

Exploring the Pattern

1st step: Find as many complete circles as possible, colour the 'petals' the same colour. The radius petals may be any choice of colour. Reverse. Working from the radius petals, find the circles . . . . . . be not deceived into leaving this out as too simple!

2nd step: Find and colour straight lines of radius 'petals' (parallels).

3rd step: Colour the petals in to show the triangles.

4th step: Draw in the straight lines of the circles to form the hexagons; rub out construction lines — the Honeycomb.

5th step: Starting with the centre hexagon, place on its sides in turn: 1. Triangles; 2. Parallelograms; 3. Rectangles; 4. Trapesia; 5. Rhombi.

Now find the 6-pointed star in the centre hexagon and place similar stars on its sides. One can now work out interlapping patterns using the sides of the central hexagon as base, and also the squares from the vesica piscis. Patterns can be arranged between these and rectangles or trapezia. The schooling of accuracy required for the intersecting circles, and the visual pleasure of the geometrical forms, make this a very satisfying task, developing mathematical 'sensing' that will be brought to consciousness in later work.

Shaded Drawing (from 7 years)

The linear pattern connects the sight-sense with the capacity of thought required for the development of general everyday intelligence.

A drawing of landscape or colour study, made by using a diagonal stroke from right to left, breaks through a thought-bound sense-percept into an imaginative element. This is often sadly lacking in our pupils, because the natural imaginative phantasy of the first years has been cut off by too much participation in conforming with grown-ups' intellectual requirements. A way to rejuvenate and call on a healthy imaginative power can be stimulated through shaded drawing. The diagonal line calls on the will element required to move 'sight' forward and back, for we ourselves have to carry our eyes in our heads towards and away from objects. The rhythmic stroke concentrates the attention, and patience is required as the picture only gradually appears. The picture can easily be made visually satisfying by the teacher.

This method of drawing can be introduced from 7 years onwards, by simple colour exercises, e.g. sequence of the rainbow colours; shading from light to dark in tones of one colour. When skill is attained, simple forms can be tried. Later we can use this method for lettering.

In classwork, introduce this shading in the sky first, gradually extending it to the whole picture. This prevents an over-emphasis of 'colouring in' with the movement of the horizontal line which emphasises the outline element, limiting the child's ability to express himself imaginatively in a visually satisfying manner.

Painting Exercises

It is important that all painting exercises are done sitting down, the position in which we write.

The Sun in the Blue Sky (from 6 years)

This motif helps the child to let go and draw himself together. It is especially helpful to those children who suddenly start lying and stealing.

Thoroughly wet the painting paper by immersing it in a bucket of water and spreading it on to an already wet board. Press out the bubbles of air and mop up excess moisture with a sponge. Mix ultramarine water-colour paint with water to a fairly deep tone, also a chrome or gamboge yellow. Starting with a good brushful of yellow, make a 'ball' in the centre of the paper, spreading out the surface and lightening the tone at the edges. Take the blue and starting from the OUTSIDE work towards the yellow, the colour becoming paler until the edges blend together (do not produce green). *Next lesson:* Repeat, starting with *blue* and leaving room for the yellow to appear. Repeat this sequence until the child can produce a balanced relationship in size and colourtone between the sun and sky by both methods.

With this accomplished the motif can be taken up again, and after the two repetitions the child may add one object to the picture, e.g. a bird. The next lesson he repeats the sun motif with the bird and adds something else — the sea, or a field — until the whole picture is composed in this way over a number of lessons.

The Blue-Red Spiral Exercise

For all children of any age: this helps to concentrate and relax, and brings about a natural harmony between in and out breathing. It may be done on an absorbent paper which has been dampened or slightly moistened. With blue paint, let the child make long unbroken strokes from left to right horizontally from the top of the paper to the bottom. Then, taking a much more concentrated amount of blue, let him start a spiral at the top left side of the paper and, moving clockwise, paint an in-going spiral. In this exercise we want to bring the movement of the spiral right up through the hand-arm movement to the shoulder. Have flat brushes so that the turning movement is easily seen. Using the broad side of the brush begin to 'draw' the spiral in one steady stroke; at the moment the turn comes to go round and below, lift the whole hand and take the movement on, each time turning the hand instead of twisting the brush between the fingers in order to keep the stroke the full width of the brush. In this way eye, hand and arm are co-ordinated into the flow of the movement (see top page 34).
Next lesson: Paint the paper red and, with a deeper red, make a spiral from the centre to the periphery, turning so that it is again a right-handed clockwise spiral. Continue to watch brush control.
3rd lesson: Paint a blue background: from inside to outside make the form of the same right-handed clockwise circle by removing the blue paint with the brush to make a clear form showing the white of the paper. Continue each movement from the beginning of the spiral to the end, then wipe the brush. In this way *the movement* is practiced; this is as important as the form and colour, provided it is done correctly — no twisting of the brush between the fingers instead of turning the whole hand and arm! Now carefully paint in from CENTRE outwards in RED. *Movement* will be anti-clockwise but the form visually is a left to right spiral.
4th lesson: Paint red background and, starting at the left hand side, make again a clockwise in-going spiral by removing the colour in continuous movement as above; then paint the form in blue.
5th lesson: Free choice from one of the preceding combinations.

Observations

Note choice of direction, starting place when painting background. There will be difficulty in mastering the brush stroke, but persevere as it has a marked effect in helping dominance problems. Repeat this exercise twice a term until a spiral is done in a easy relaxed manner.

Secondary Colour Exercise (from 11 years; see illustrations on page 84)

To help Spatial Orientation: to help in relation to Body Geography.
    Give the child the choice of painting with either Purple, Orange or Green. With chosen colour (orange), cover the paper using long rhythmic strokes, left to right horizontally, one laid next to and slightly over-lapping the other. Now ask what colours are hidden in the orange. Red and yellow.
    On a fresh sheet of damp paper paint these colours side by side — one half of the paper, yellow, the other half, red (child's choice for colours and painting direction). Left-right now becomes visible in coloured planes.
Next lesson: Repeat the orange background. On second paper, paint red/ yellow above-below (child's choice of colour for above and below).
3rd lesson: Repeat the orange background. Second painting, one colour inside, surrounded by the other.
4th lesson: Repeat the orange background. Paint from opposite corners so that the right to left diagonal appears, or start from centre diagonal and paint to opposite corners (free choice).
5th lesson: Make a picture or a form, using all three colours.

Observations

Especially good for the withdrawn, tense child and the complacent undisturbable child.
    The repetition of this exercise is essential. Note how 'stuck' to one colour the child is: when he changes his choice freely the exercise has worked. Repeat again at a good interval, either to check his response, or should he become 'stuck' at another stage of development.

Blue/Red 'Perspective' Exercise (from 11 years)

To cultivate inner awareness of spatial relationship. *Do not use* before eleven years of age. See diagram drawings on facing page.
    Use the largest size sheets of damp paper (75 cm x 55 cm) for these

exercises. Prepare two jam jars, one with ultramarine water colour paint, diluted with water but keeping it a strong tone; prepare the other jar with carmine or crimson lake. Have a broad paint brush in each jar. The pupil is to paint with long unbroken strokes of paint, placing each next to the other without gaps. He paints first a stroke with one colour in the given direction. He returns the brush to the jar and takes the brush from the other jar and paints in the given direction so that a diagonal line formed by the two colours gradually appears across the paper*. *(Paint using one hand only)*.

Observations

This is especially good for the scattered, unconcentrated child; for children who cannot recall events to mind easily. Also for children who have had shocks in early childhood which have made them 'mother clingers'. For children who have to travel long distances by air in the holidays.

    The children paint these exercises with great care and intensity of concentration, especially the older ones.

    Version L is the main exercise for use generally.

    Version M should be added for those children who cannot keep the left foot under control in the Ball Twirling Exercise. Use a rhythm of 3 : 1.

    Use versions N and O (as required) in the same way.

Movement Directions for the Blue-Red Perspective Exercise

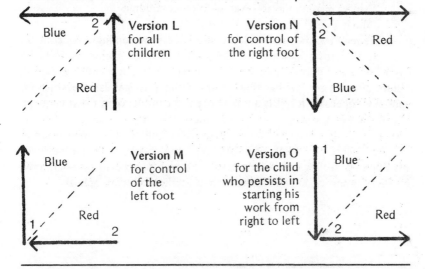

* Observe two or three lessons before making any corrections

These are also important for children who 'choose' with the left hand and pass the object over to the right hand for use.

In those instances where we observe the child persistently starting to paint from the right side of the paper to the left — sometimes with vertical strokes, we should try and help with version O. Medically considered, this is one of the symptoms of minimal brain damage; we can try to give the individuality help in forming compensatory orientation by such exercises as this — 'O' 3x; 'M' 1x weekly; or concentrated periods daily for a week. *Note:* The numbering and movement sequences of the Right-angle Triangle and Blue/Red Painting Exercises have been chosen in accordance with laws indicated by Rudolf Steiner*. Note that on the two-dimensional plane, the current of the astral (soul) body runs at right angles to those of the life/physical bodies.

Results

The comments which colleagues make after a term's work run somewhat as follows:

"He's much better."

"Not such a nuisance in the classroom."

"Quite a different attitude."

"At least *now* he tries to do something."

"Not so restless and aggravating to other children."

"Much quieter, but he can't read yet!"

We may take heart; at least the 'side effects' are coming under control!

Such changes indicate that the growing, living forces in the child are assimilating and transforming what we do with him. Our eventual success or failure depends on whether there is any actual physical damage which we cannot compensate for; it is our patience and confidence in the strengthening of the will through rhythmic repetition which will stimulate the healing forces. If we give the child those things which belong to the foundation of his intelligence-producing organism, his astral body, then the basis for his thinking, feeling and willing eventually will be brought into harmony, his health improve and comprehension of intellectual work appear.

---

* *Anthroposophy*, 1909, Chapter 1

Chapter Five

THE RE-INTRODUCTION TO FORMAL WORK
IN READING AND ARITHMETIC

Reading Develops Through a Living Relationship to Writing

The early mastery of reading is the accomplishment which gives parents the greatest satisfaction and separates, in their estimation, the "clever" child from the slow.

The norms of our educational pattern require teachers to conform to an early reading proficiency, although research projects have shown that a child of 6-plus develops in a short time the capacity which it takes a child twice as long to achieve when the starting age is 5.

Most children have the ability to respond to the teaching methods of today and comply with the accepted norms: whether this is to the best advantage for their health in later years forms an important part of the discussion between Rudolf Steiner and teachers.

Those children who are in difficulties with their reading need to recapitulate the way in which mankind as a whole came to acquire the art of writing and then reading.

Repetition underlies all growth and flowering from plant and animal to all the functions of the human being. We are all born, change our teeth, go through puberty and become adult, so there is every reason to repeat in miniature the historical sequence by which reading developed from pictures to signs. We wrote and then read what we had written down*.

The situation of the child who comes to us is that at some level the unrelated sound to the *form* of the letter has been rejected by his consciousness — b for bat — the symbol has no relation to the form of the object whatever, for this is a mnemonic aid only.

It is the object which he sees that is real to the child and so he has refused to relate and remember: the whole process is mixed up with contradictory feelings — bewilderment, fear, resentment at not being able to meet the adults' requirements, the other children's attitudes, his own ineptitude; we can well understand why emotionally he oscillates between frustration and lack of interest. To release him from this

---

* Steiner, R. *Human Values in Education.* Arnheim 1924, page 61

situation we must make the symbol, its sound and movement, coalesce into a unity and become a picture of itself.

wave   valley   mountains

We have to exert our phantasy for some of our sound/symbols.

Tree: the branches can be weighted down with fruit.

Presenting the first · elements of reading in this way has never failed to interest the 12-year olds. Having made clear the process they could, by their own phantasy, turn most of the letters into pictures from which they then wrote a story. Some were able to write it down, others dictated their story. It was then written out for them in clear copperplate writing. This they had to copy out in 'painting' writing, using a folded sheet of 75 cm x 55 cm sized paper. The first page was kept as the cover and a part of each lesson was spent making a design with the 'pictures' illustrating the story. Inside, lines were drawn a ruler's width apart — our pupils are not skilled and an hour flies by — then with the finest possible paint brush, size 00 — this adds lustre to the task — they paintily wrote. From a therapy point of view this requires a complete change in movement habit — holding the brush and keeping it suspended requires new muscles to be brought into play. The child is interested, hand and eye work together in a new way and by the time we finish this operation the antipathy to print and writing is overcome. No pictorial records remain of such work, as this has been the one thing that no one ever left behind!

In view of the reading methods which some children have experienced before coming to us, it is essential that any child of any age should experience the letters as pictures. Children under age 12 should have them introduced by the teacher. After that age the child's phantasy is active and he can make his own as described above. It is essential to overcome the subconscious fear of print — of the unknown at work in the soul. It is this fear which makes for inaccurate and superficial reading and consequent memory re-call problems.

Children with cross dominance between eye and hand were given glasses-frames without lenses and the offending eye had to look through a lens of blue lighting gelatine, if it was the left eye, or red, if it was the

LETTER STORY

Composed by a boy in Class 9 and written out with the paintbrush method.

He came during Class 8 because his handwriting was illegible, his reading very limited and he was unable to express himself in language. This exercise concluded our work together, and in the words of the final sentence: "Everything was all right again".

Princess Idonia goes up the mountain to a hermit who lives in a cave. In anger he changes Idonia into a squirrel and he then decides to give her a tree in his valley.

One day, a prince came to the King and found out that the princess had disappeared. He set out to find her. An eagle tells him how it caught a fish, and the fish, in exchange for his life, told him this story. . .The fish had been swimming in a river and had seen the hermit in a boat. The hermit had been muttering to himself that only an opal found in snow over which the waves of the sea washed would, when shown to the squirrel, bring Idonia into her shape.

For seven years he searched for the opal, but in the end it was found in the snow white bed of pearls over which the waves of the sea had washed.

Helped by the eagle, he found the hermit and overcame the hermit's anger by giving him the opal.

Everything was all right again.

right eye. In this way the uncovered eye was brought into activity and developed the required dominance.

The children were free to paint in any colour. Some changed the colour at every word until they became aware of the sentence. Others used, for a time, a new colour for each line. It was interesting to see how sentence comprehension grew by the end of the story. A suitable precis had been made to fill the three pages. Occasionally certain details were insisted upon and then another page was added. Each lesson, the part of the story already written was read aloud from the copy. . .the pupil had to take a step on each word and turn and go in the opposite direction at a full stop. While this project was on hand, part of the homework was to make the capital letters in the shaded drawing technique, proceeding from these to the whole word. Next, only the capital letters were shaded; finally the word was written in ordinary writing. In this way the necessary repetition was achieved. This work can lead quite naturally to copying out word lists from F. Schonell's excellent book, or to whatever style of formal work the teacher considers suitable.

We can help bad writing and immobility of looking by making the eye use unaccustomed movements when writing. Children can be helped to *see* spelling if they write — 'Chinese' or 'Greek'.

Take a well-known poem or even nursery rhyme and, starting on the right side of the page, write it from above downwards — letters under each other. Then write in the Greek "Boustrophedon" from right to left and left to right, even turning the letters!

One very 'protest' left-handed dyslexic boy, with illegible handwriting and no interest in writing, at last thought he would not mind writing in Egyptian. The hieroglyphics for Ramses, Thutmosis and Scribe were duly conned and he was told to paint a background of blue on the largest size moist paper, leaving out the forms of the hieroglyphics; these were painted in afterwards in red. This obliged him to hold the picture of the form in his mind's eye while painting in the background. When completed he now had something he could read which no one else could! Later he taught himself to write beautifully. Such things are by no means avoiding the issue. Interest awakens inner movement, which is the first step towards comprehension. Painting words and sentences in this manner is also helpful at some stages of development.

Reading Aloud

We now have to tackle the problem of reading aloud. This requires retention of content and quick comprehension if it is to be of any satisfaction to reader and listener. To prepare this capacity a number of exercises will be described which rouse in the child the relationship of the senses one to another. These exercises are for use on a daily basis during a period of remedial work. As all sense activity is heightened by the loss of sight, we will blindfold our pupil (or paint over the glass of bathing goggles), and give him some of the following tasks:

(1) Threading beads: threading them in a given shape pattern; guessing the number he has threaded; handling objects and identifying them; feeling objects with the feet, etc.; listening to and identifying sounds — from which direction have they come. . .high up, the next room, from below. . ,?; Knitting, crochet, modelling, plaiting and knotting; distinguishing the seven tastes — sweet, sour, sharp, bitter, salty, spicy, hot; describing surfaces and textures.

(2) Exercises *to lead from observation to thinking*

"Close your eyes and name five things in the room" — increase the number each time. "What is on the left side of the door as you come in?". "How many people did you pass on the way to school?". "Is there a tree at the school gate?".

To link observation to memory, ask:

"What was I wearing yesterday?". "What colour is Mr. X's tie today — yesterday?". "What has been changed in the room?". "What has been added to it?".

To stimulate the memory:

We can ask a simple question and tell the pupil to hold back the answer and give it next day. The question must be so obvious that the answer is immediately there, e.g. "How many legs has a cow?".

To help the child to form concepts:

Make him describe something for you to guess without naming it. Then he must guess what you describe. Let him choose something and describe it in one word, then two words, three words, etc., or "How many objects in the room begin with the same letter?".

To help the sense of hearing:

Sit with the pupil in silence and then ask how many sounds he has heard, naming them, saying where they have come from and how they have been caused.

We can play the intervals and the scale on the lyre, asking the pupil to show how they rise and fall by the movement of his arms. Let him hear a rhythm on one note; he must clap it, walk it, and also play it. Let him find words that fit a rhythm and discover the rhythm in a word. This can be extended to a sentence. The child should acquire the skill to hear a rhythm once and then be able to walk it and beat it on a drum or tambourine. See that the hexameter is mastered in this way.

To make a relationship between hearing, movement and sight:

We can do the following: we say a number, e.g. 12, and ask the child what the number will be when he has paced to the door. He must assess this and see if he is right by stepping and counting from 12 until he has reached the door, and then tell us how many steps he has taken.

When a certain amount of skill and confidence has been gained, we can begin the direct approach to reading.

A new picture of reading aloud has to be formed. Has the child a sense of drama? Has he begun to enjoy words? Is he the shy, withdrawn type for whom it is agony to open his mouth and let out a sound? With the former children Tacitus' *Agricola* is splendid reading. It is meant to be read to an audience, so set the scene and explain the context of the reading. Then, standing side by side with the book (English translation, of course!) on a music stand, you declaim the first sentence with your pupil pointing for you; you make him keep up with you. Then he has to read the same sentence — he can't, of course — so you whisper it as he goes along and he speaks and points. So you proceed thus for a few minutes. We shall have the shock of discovering how poor is the connection between hearing and memory. The important thing is the enjoyment, the grand swing of the sentence, the pronouncing of new lush-sounding words. This is the real thing at last and what reading is about!

The tense child will be happier with Julius Caesar. Neat, curt sentences, saying exactly what is meant.

When confidence is established and he is pointing for your reading, stop suddenly and let him say the word: be sure it is one he knows or can read phonetically. Conversely name a difficult word on the page and let him find it.

The reader who constantly looks up can be helped by taking a piece of paper and cutting a window in it, placing it on the page so that a word appears in it. Then cover the word and let the child say it.

To help children between 6 and 8 years

Write out a well-known rhyme. Let the children read it through, then recognise a line, then a word in a line, and finally a letter in a word.

We can help to break tenseness in reading habits and the hold of the attention on to the unknown word, or the over-concentration on phonetic pronunciation by developing 'rhythmic reading'.

Stage 1: Take a postcard and cover the reading matter except for the group of words or sentence which the pupil is to read. He reads it silently, pointing with his finger, then he reads it aloud, still pointing: continue like this through the story;

Stage 2: He reads silently the portion shown; it is covered and he says it aloud;

Stage 3: He reads silently, the sentence is covered; he says it aloud, then writes down the sentence and checks it from his book.

Stage 1 should be worked at until the child is at ease before proceeding to the other stages. This method overcomes the shallow breathing caused by tension, allows an understanding of time to develop, and a rhythm is set up between breath and comprehension. Memory and writing can then be developed.

For older children, 15 – 18 years, who have weak reading ability

Set a given time for them to read a passage. At the end of the time they must say in one word what the passage is about; then say it in two words; then three words. *This develops thought content.*

Arithmetic

This subject too requires the ability to move: here it is an inward concentration which gives rise to a movement from one part of a process to the next. This faculty is lacking in our pupil; it is also lacking in his physical movements. He is the child who cannot keep in step with others. These children are surprised that their agility to move does not fit in with their imagination of their capacity.

The lessons for these pupils should consist of those movement exercises to which counting and tables can be said aloud: the stepping exercise relating movement and hearing given above, and the Counting Star. Check his dominance and confirm it with the Right-angle Triangle Exercise. Use the Copper Ball or Rod-rolling Exercise for relaxation of tension, and for the development between aural and visual centres.

We can develop the connection between sight and concept through extending the 'Bean counting' assessment. He should guess how many beans altogether in the pile — separate them out and decide how many red and how many blue. He then counts both. Another time he counts the total and sorts them into two heaps: he guesses one pile, counts the other, and corrects his guess with the total.

Make many variations of this, starting with a known number and separating it into various piles, one of which remains uncounted and has to be calculated from the number in the others. This creates confidence. We can also use this method with the other three processes*.

It is quite common for the 12-year olds still not to have grasped how units, 10s, 100s, are formed: also how numbers are composed and written down. So return to the basic 'carrying' concept by using pints, quarts and gallons — practically, at the kitchen sink with jug, bottle and bucket. When this is grasped, practise writing it down in reduction sums forward and back. From this, explain units, tens and hundreds and practise writing answers in words. This overcomes fear. Being unable to grasp number concepts always induces tenseness and fear of the unknown. . . in the child this gives the effect of being slow or stupid in reaction.

We can also help this emotional attitude to dissolve by speaking of the quality of numbers, their relationship to the body and to form. The number one is whole and indivisible. He is one person, but two is contained in his two eyes, two arms, etc. Also in him is expressed 'Threeness', head, trunk and limbs etc. This gives confidence.

We can lead over from the Counting Star to geometrical forms. Let him draw an equilateral triangle, freehand, very large, and divide the sides into equal parts. Number the parts on the base, continue on to the next side but start at one again. Start at one on the third side. Now join all the ones, twos, etc., in freehand, and a central circle formed by the straight

---

* Steiner, R. *Discussions with Teachers.* Stuttgart 1919. Page 44

lines should appear! Adapt with pentagram and hexagram. This rhythmic counting, the forms, the accuracy, build up the badly needed confidence and pleasure in the beauty of numbers (see page 85).

We can use all four rules and long division by reduction sums (both ways). Alas only 'years to seconds' seem left to us. Then the converse 'millions of seconds' into minutes, hours, days, months, years! No short cuts. When the pupil can run up and down this 'ladder' easily we can tackle the fractions.

Take a sheet of paper and let him tear it in two. That cannot be done to him! His 'one' is a whole, so are all the parts. Now he meets a condition where numbers are less than one: but in fractions we see that each part is equal. Let him fold the paper equally and tear it. Pass on to drawing circles and divide them equally from halves to twelfths, etc. He is to colour in the required fraction from the numerator: 3/4; 7/12; soon the mystery of 3/4 and 6/8 will dawn on him. As a grand finale, make a Victoria sponge cake together and fractionise slices, eating them as this is done.

The reader may feel he has had a surfeit of exercises, many of which are saying the same thing in another form. This is so, but repetition strengthens the will and cultivates memory, faculties our pupil desperately needs. As teachers, we must develop phantasy and imagination so that our pupil is challenged and surprised; this enables the continual repetition of the basic therapy to be carried through.

As a 15-year old loftily remarked at the end of two years' work "I shouldn't have come if I hadn't liked the things you did with me.".

Chapter Six

ORGANISING LESSONS

Structure and Timing of Lessons

The quality of the time the pupil spends with us is as important as the instruction we have to give. There must be no sense of pressure or of the 'importance of getting on'.

We can introduce our method of working to our younger pupils of 11 — 12 years of age by describing how the farmer first of all prepares his fields before he sows his wheat, and then tell him that we are going to do the same kind of thing, and if we do it thoroughly then the writing will come naturally.

For the older pupil of 13 onwards, we can say straight out to him that reading is a matter of movement; that the whole form of the letter and word has to be moved through by the eye and, like a lightning-flash, penetrate the whole body and be reflected to him, in his mind. In our lessons together we shall explore all 'kinds' of movement to see what is obstructing the 'flash'.

The children are both puzzled and relieved, interest is aroused and their own inability to do many of the exercises intrigues and challenges them. When circumstances permit, it is better for our pupil that no formal reading is done for at least two terms, for if the system has refused to assimilate and correlate information, and the child cannot produce at will what he is supposed to know, then saturation point within the organism has been reached and there is no point in pressing on this weakness with further demands, deepening it and maybe causing other troubles. We must aim at supporting and cultivating complementary parts of the body, with its supersensible members, so that growth of faculty is stimulated.

The lesson should be composed so that all the elements discussed are represented — Body Geography, Spatial Orientation — Dominance, etc., and they should be cultivated from each aspect: movement — drawing — painting.

The basic exercise which should be included in every lesson is the Copper Ball Exercise, followed by the Moving Straight Line and Lemniscate; around these the other exercises are composed. The Rod-rolling Exercise is a must for pale weak children; for those who are withdrawn; for those with poor shallow breathing. When the eye dominance has to be changed the Counting Star must be practised regularly, with the wrong dominant eye covered in the appropriate colour. *All lessons should end with a painting exercise.*

The Right-angle Triangle Exercise should be started in the second term and done consistently for at least a term at the weekly lesson! When formal work has begun this exercise should be continued.

Example of a Work Programme (when the lesson is given once a week):

Rod Rolling; Marbles between toes; Ball Throwing; practice of Flower Rod Exercise or Counting Star; Copper Ball Exercise and Moving Lemniscate; one exercise blindfold and a painting exercise (1 hour).

The lesson should be so composed that it is an artistic experience for the pupil. The teacher could base his choice of exercises on the principle of 'in and out' breathing, expansion-contraction element, or through using the three soul faculties of thinking, feeling and will. Some musical element, for example recognising and playing the intervals on a glockenspiel, can awaken consciousness and help cultivate listening. This can complement the painting exercises.

For children starting lessons who are already 15 — 18 years old and *want* to read, we can introduce some of the formal work as soon as there is skill in form work, mirror patterns, etc. They can begin with the letters as 'pictures' composing their own story from them, shading the capital letters; conversely shading a background colour so that the form of a letter appears, then colouring it in. Words can be done in the same way.

To Call Up Inner Visualization:

Write letters and then words on the pupil's back with a finger, or with a feather on the palm of his hand, letting him write them at the same time into his book and reading them. Let him choose a word which is then written on his back while he again writes it down. *But Movement Exercises and painting must be maintained and comprise the greater part of the lesson.*

Homework (this is a must — ten minutes a day)

Part of the first lessons have to be spent in building up a homework programme. This will consist of form and pattern drawing and a colour exercise in shaded drawing: also modelling in beeswax or plasticine. Whether or not their contemporaries are having a full homework programme, our pupils should have a specific handwork task. Knitting is an important function for concentration and Eye-Hand Co-ordination, plus counting and concept forming. So pupils of 13 onwards — and they have mostly been boys — have had to make themselves a pullover in quick knit, a specific amount to be done each week. This is a third or fourth term programme. Making a set of table mats or a rug in Finger Knitting* is also valuable for its therapeutic effect on the stiff 'stretching movements': at least one table mat in this technique should be made during the course of our work.

When mastered, the Flower-Rod Exercise, drawing interpenetrating triangles, triangle and circle expansion and contraction, the various 'counting forms', are all homework material. Later, word lists, and sentence-making from them, can be added. Our pupils should also have to complete dramatic incidents which are read or described; also to complete stories which they are reading, comparing their ending with the actual one.

Re-assessment: Monitoring Progress

The Cross Test: at the end of the third term or beginning of the next school year.
Flower Rod: not necessary as it is a therapy exercise and is practised until it is correct and fluently done.
Bean-counting: not necessary if used as a therapy exercise. Can be used to re-check hand dominance and speech movement co-ordination at the beginning of third term or commencement of new short session period.
Dominance: simple check at the end of second term. Handedness Assessment at the end of third term.
Eye-Colour Affinity: twice or even three times during the term. If a child starts to personify the sun and moon by giving them faces and characters, continue giving opportunity for this week by week until he stops. The 'story' and pictures show that tensions and habits are being thrown off. This is rare but not to be thwarted should it occur. Be casual in manner when giving this assessment, slipping it in at the end of a lesson when there's 'no time' for a whole picture. Only two children have recognised this as an assessment and the answer given was the characterization already mentioned — 'whether the pupil is riding the horse or carrying it', but not, of course, letting him know which he is doing!

---

* Macdonald, E.M., *Cord Knotting.* Dryad Leaflet No. 127

We have to recognise that our work is producing a cleansing process in our pupil, so we must not be surprised when he goes through a crisis. His disability is a form of protest and at some point he and we are bound to bump up against this and wrestle with it. One senses this moment as a concealed obstinacy and it is our skilful use of the exercises that frees his forces so that faculty develops. The Eye Colour Affinity assessment indicates when we are 'touching' on the 'blockages'. Suddenly, after two or three correct versions, reversal may occur: the colour choice of the red may change to vermilion, or blue and yellow be taken instead – this often occurs and afterwards the path of development smooths out and consistent correct colour affinity is maintained.

As experience grows we 'sense' when such processes are occurring and can use the assessment to confirm or question what stage the pupil is going through. If progress is 'stuck' this will show us why. The Right-angle Triangle Exercise is a great 'releaser'. With careful observation we may note that the pupil is too facile in his movement when doing this exercise or that the *non*-dominant eye has an immobile look. We may then try to free forces by giving our pupil the 'opposite' pattern of this exercise – the left, for the right-handed child, and the right-hand version to the left-hander*. (Four to six times if the lesson is weekly; for two – three weeks if the lessons are daily, and then check with the Eye Colour Affinity). The Blue-Red perspective painting exercise should be added if there is no result.

The Use of the Exercises for Classes or Groups

Writing (6 – 9 years)

The method of introducing the letters as pictures can be used from the age of six**; in this case the teacher uses his imagination to invent the pictures and compose the story. In this way the consonants are easily recognised as 'shaping sounds' and the vowels as the 'singing sounds' which each word needs. Owing to the complication of English spelling, the vowels need to be introduced by pictures of their name – as in 'eagle' – as well as by their sound, which has the gesture of a feeling quality. Oh – O – surprise; OO – awe. Children can act the 'long' or naming sounds of the vowels; their shortened version can be imitated with little jumps and miniature gesture.

The use of capital letters for writing before the cursive small letters

---

* See pages 35 – 38
** Steiner, R. *Practical Course for Teachers.* Stuttgart, 1919

is important. The form of the capital letters brings about the law which is the basis of evolution — repetition before the new accomplishment can be produced — in this instance the repetition of the spatial orientation the child has achieved during the first 5 — 6 years of his life. Examination of children's drawings shows the order in which above-below, left-right symmetry and the diagonal is accomplished: this is the effect of the sense percepts and movement of the body in three-dimensional space. At a new stage of development, after the change of teeth for example, this has to be re-acquired as an inner visual capacity. What better, more real, practice can we give the child to do than to copy stories in capital letters?

Every time he draws 'T', he neatly divides space into left-right with the down stroke; into above-below with the horizontal bar above the 'T'. In the letter 'K' we have left-right space in connection with the diagonal forward-back, when the strokes are made to and from the first assertive down stroke.

Our capital letters are composed of the two fundamental forms of geometry, the straight line and circle (curve).

Here we practice something of infinite value for inner conceptual imaginative vision as the 'pictures' of the letters are still connected with their form and so enjoyed in the writing thereof. A stilted vocabulary need not be used; a long word is full of 'pictures' in itself, and repetition soon develops the memory faculty. Reading aloud from the board, and writing as a class and alone, leads to confident expressive reading. While this stage is being worked at, preparation is made for the small case and cursive writing through pattern drawing, mirror forms, etc.

At this stage all the Body Geography Exercises should be used. Basic body geography is contained in all the children's singing games which have been collected and appear in so many excellent editions. It is the writer's opinion that it has been these games, played so rhythmically in their seasonal activity, which 'cured' the mixed dominance and poor body geography of earlier childhoods. Now that their spontaneous use is dying away, more and more educators are incorporating them into their curricula.

General Exercises

Movement: all ball-throwing examples — left-right, above-below orientation; Rod-rolling; Marbles Between the Toes; 'Stretching and Lifting' Exercise (very good for concentrating attention of a class before the lesson); clapping and walking rhythms; walking and stepping to sentences or numbers, saying them forward and then backward, step on each word or number.

Drawing (6 — 7 years): cursive patterns (introduce as given for Eye Hand Co-ordination, etc.); The Counting Star.

7 years and over

Drawing: Mirroring on vertical and horizontal axis and in circular repetition and palindrome. Introduce shaded drawings for 'skies' in their drawings. Painting: The Blue-Red Spiral. This should be done once a term, either the daily rhythm or one part of the exercise each week. Done on damp paper with paints already mixed, it is intended only to use 10 — 15 minutes of the lesson.

For children who have difficulty in maintaining the right-hand spiral when left free, a period of the three-fold spiral as an individual exercise should be done before school or incorporated into a free activity period.

The Sun in the Blue Sky motif as a story sequence.

From 9 years

Drawing: Spatial Lemniscates; area exercise. Illustrated drawings should now be done in the shaded technique.
Painting: The Secondary Colour Exercise.

From 11 years

Movement: The Copper Ball Exercise (in gym groups); hexameter — stepping and clapping.
Drawing: Interpenetrating triangles; geometry of the hexagon.
Painting: The Blue-Red Perspective Exercise sequences, versions L and M. Especially helpful in classes where many children are having long journeys each day — minimum once a week.

Assessment for Classes

On entry from 6 years (see page 20)

To enter Class One, the child must be six years of age at the commencement of the Autumn term. It has been the practice to persuade parents of children whose birthdays are so near this deadline to allow the children another year in the kindergarten. When this has been done, the benefits have always been apparent. With the increasing life-tempo and sensory impacts, children are less and less ready for school life at 6 years; they need another six months to fully complete the last stage of the kindergarten development.

From 7 years — to the assessments on pages 20 and 21, add:

Handedness Pattern Assessment (page 13)
Flower-Rod Exercise (page 14)
Mirroring Test (page 16)

[The straight and wavy line, figure-of-8 and flower form (page 20), can be used at the teacher's discretion after class 2].

Re-check at 9 years, and 11 — 12 years, with:

Cross Test.
Eye Colour Affinity.
Flower-Rod.
Dominance and Handedness Assessments if changed earlier.

In this way, teachers can keep track of the general constitutional progress of their pupils and anticipate troubles likely to arise at puberty, by taking appropriate action in time to give them the necessary help and support.

CONCLUSION

Basic Forms (Archetypes)

Geometry and mathematics have been the educators of mankind's intelligence throughout historical development, awakening him to his unique place in the created world. The ability to grasp the basic forms, visually and inwardly, has led to the achievements of past civilisations and to the development of modern consciousness. For example, in the form of the spiral we have all the directions of space contained in movement — left-right, above-below, in-out, forward and back. It is easy to draw a spiral from outside to the centre. If we want to draw the same spiral from inside to outside we have to notice carefully which way to go: if we do not notice whether we start on the left or right, and go above when we should go below, we end up with the spiral drawn in the reverse direction as in a mirror. This wonderful movement of the spiral we find everywhere in nature and today in many a domestic machine.

These basic forms which have accompanied mankind are constantly being re-discovered and re-applied, from the $2 - 3$ relationship of area to volume which led to "iron" ships, to the neat use of parallelograms on which lavatory paper is wound. They raise man's thinking to eternal truths and at the same time make him master of the earth.

Confronted with such forms, the child senses these qualities; they relate him to his past and bring him into relationship with the true and beautiful. Making these forms calls on the inner intelligence hidden in each human being.

The remedial factor today must be one that helps the individual to establish his identity in face of whatever type of heredity he possesses and the environmental situation in which life has placed him. Then he will develop the faculty to retain for tomorrow what he has learnt today.

APPENDIX

Handedness Assessment Forms

For Children from Seven Years (first use the circle, then the forms below)

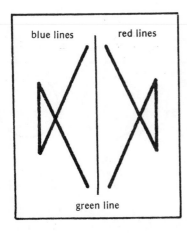 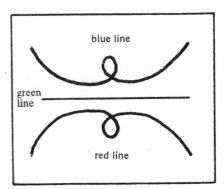

Note: Children to not follow the green lines

For Children from Eleven Years (first use the circle, then the forms below)

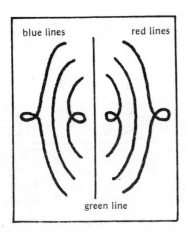 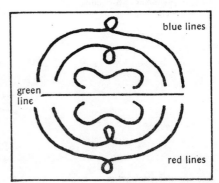

Handedness

Over Seven Years

Dominance:

Eye:

Foot:

Hand:

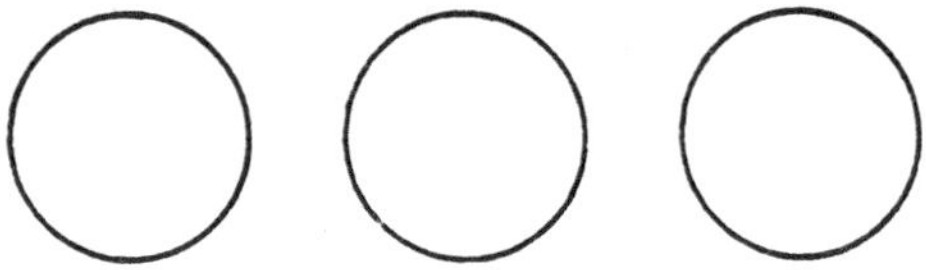

Both Feet | One Foot | Foot-Hand

Notes:

Arrows for direction of movement; dot starting place on each side of form — show first side with x or 1;
s — simultaneous use of hand, feet or foot-hand;
over form shows that crossing line was not followed;
— loop added after drawing the form;
h — eye covered by hand;
m — eye closed muscularly.

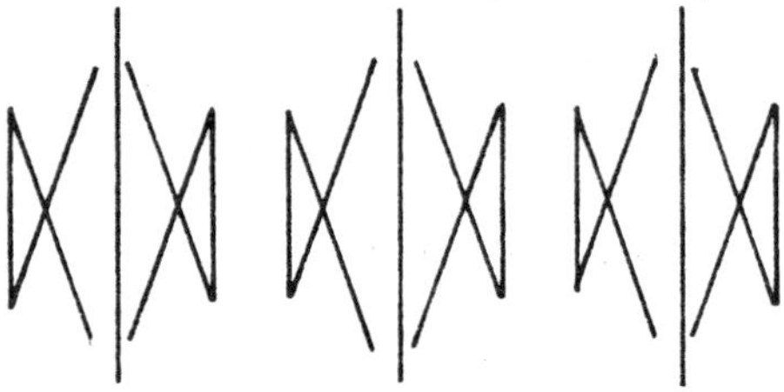

Both Feet | One Foot | Foot-Hand

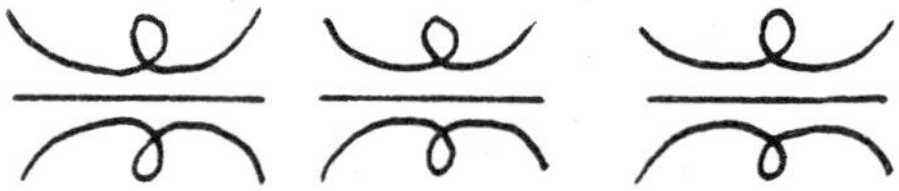

Both Feet | One Foot | Foot-Hand

Special Remarks:

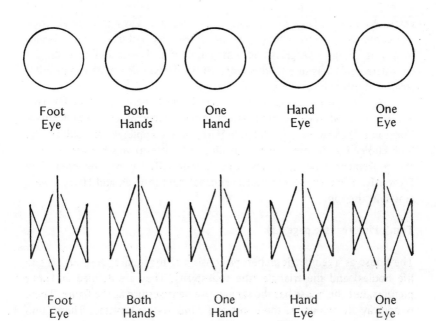

| Foot | Both | One | Hand | One |
| Eye | Hands | Hand | Eye | Eye |

| Foot | Both | One | Hand | One |
| Eye | Hands | Hand | Eye | Eye |

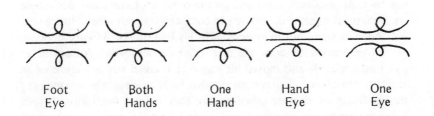

| Foot | Both | One | Hand | One |
| Eye | Hands | Hand | Eye | Eye |

INTERPRETATION OF MAN, HOUSE, TREE DRAWINGS

Introduction

It is to be understood that the following indications for 'reading' the Man, House, Tree pictures apply only when the drawings have been done in the following conditions: at the end of an assessment and preceded by the spatial-clapping sequence (see page 20).

The following pictures are by three boys, let us call them Tom (7 years, 9 months), Dick (10 years, 4 months), and Harry (12 years). Dick had come from a state school a year previously. He had made a good beginning, but stopped progress and was withdrawn. The school psychologist considered this was due to the shock of his friend's death, and to hospital treatment after an accident.

Tom's writing was large and uncertain, with many reversals. The two other boys used very pointed letters, and in Harry's case it was illegible. Tom and Dick were cross-lateral; Harry was completely left-sided. The limb choice by all three (in the Handedness Pattern) was bizarre, as were the movement sequences. The Eye Colour Affinity was reversed. The Flower-Rod exercises were 'bottle-necked', and in Dick and Harry's were closed at the top.

Tom's Pictures (see page 75)

The house as a geometric archetype consists of the square (the physical and life bodies) and the triangle (the soul-spirit). They are defined in Tom's pictures, but the house has the same movement gesture as the figure. There is no way in or out, as the doors and windows are omitted. There is no smoke coming from the chimney.

The man does not show the completed development of the pre-school stage; head — upper body and arms — lower body and legs. Here the body is a rectangle, and the arms come out at awkward angles as though on one side he feels the Greek cross and on the other the Latin cross. Both these are archetypal stages and, here, are in conflict with each other. Notice how red and blue stand out in reversal as in his Eye Colour Affinity drawing.

Tom started to draw the man from the legs which jut out at an awkward angle. He also moved his legs in an unusual way as a result of an accident. His choice of purple shows that he is aware of the streaming of the life-forces which were called-on, but they did not reach into his feet. There are hands, but they are drawn at the 5-year-old stage. On the surface,

the hat would appear the most natural thing for a child to draw, but experience tells otherwise: it indicates that there is some blockage of the formative forces in their streaming from the head into the body.

The tree, as archetype, is connected with the many functions of the rhythmic system — in this instance, its structure. There are no leaves, so the soul is not impinging strongly enough, and the gesture of the branches is erratic.

Spatially, the picture is immature. Above and below are only indicated. There is a suggestion of 'forward and back' from the position of the man, but he is hemmed-in by the house and tree. We have a picture of an arrested 5-year-old development.

The enigmatic point in the first drawing is the hook drawn in the neck. On enquiry, we learned that Tom had fallen out of bed and broken his jaw when he was 5 years old. It was suggested that Tom be seen by an Osteopath, and the examination showed that the injury to the jaw had resulted in a maladjustment which was causing a subtle disfunction in the nervous system.

Picture no. 2 (a year later). No remediation had been done in addition to the work of the Class teacher. The figure, tree and house have all changed. The most development is shown in the house (the body). Smoke comes from the chimney, and the house now has a window. Windows are a connecting link between the inner and outer experiences of the senses; their number also tells us how the soul life expresses its connection. This one window shows that the soul has to find its way into the body via the forces connected with the solar plexus. There is no cross in the window, so the sense impressions are overwhelming the soul; the fresh life-forces (purple) are still held back by the violet.

Dick's Pictures (see page 77)

Dick's picture is very impoverished, even after a year at a Waldorf School. There is no sky, only a line of earth. Man, house and tree come right to the edge of the paper, so that there is no 'forward-back' spatial element of the Will. The tree is the 'life-line', and even that is weak. It portrays the way into the breathing organization — the passages of the air — but only tenuously. The lung area shows itself in the surrounding green.

The house is only 'half-present'. This is becoming a more frequent motif. There is no real archetype imprint, neither are the roof and walls differentiated. There is one window with a rough cross. Although merged

into the house, the soul is trying to protect itself from being overwhelmed with sense impressions. Both house and figure are in the dark brown. Children use this colour when they are over-weighed by 'old forces', for example: strongly working heredity from the past, old habits and instincts, etc.

Again the figure is very primitive — not even a natural 'young-stage' type. There are no hands or feet, and only the mouth (jaw) is differentiated. Note Steiner's observation that the lower jaw and its muscular system receives everything that pours spiritually from the head. (Speech and Drama Course, 1923). Now look at the set of the head on the neck and the arms. Learning of his accident, we again asked for a structural check. In this case, x-ray showed that a vertebrae was displaced in the shoulder region. After treatment, Dick said, "O mummy, now I feel so free!". Extra Lesson Work was continued, so that the bodily co-ordination could be 're-educated', and the other needed help given.

The second picture was done a year later (fourth in a very interesting series). The three dimensional space is now present. The tree is flourishing. The triangle of the roof to the walls is there. The brown has changed in this and the tree to the lighter shade. The two windows tell us that the soul is busy transforming the two-fold hereditary body (head-trunk). The door has a knob AND a window. In an earlier drawing, the inset colours were blue and red. The purple of the new life forces is in full 'swing' in house and garden. A pathway to the door has appeared, and a figure approaches; it is of a woman. (Students who have read *The Education of the Child in the Light of Anthroposophy* will understand this). Dick is not quite through into the physical body with his will forces; there is no chimney yet, but the sun is shining, the figure has hands and feet, and the violet element (a colour which always denotes soul strain or anxiety) is being changed into the true purple of the life forces.

These first four drawings (pages 75 and 77) were deliberately chosen to demonstrate the objectivity of the picture, when it has been done after the required preliminary conditions.

Harry's Pictures (see page 79)

Spatial orientation is shown to some extent; left-right being weak. Sidedness has not been firmly established; the tree dominates the picture. It is an 'airy' tree, its roots just touching the ground. Here we are seeing the impact of the breath (soul) on its vehicle of the nerve-sense system. The pronounced 'greenness' is a sign of the intellectual element. Harry always

had an answer. He knew where anybody and anything was at home, but couldn't find his own nose.

The house is 'hollow', the windows floating in the walls (note they are purple, the door red). The structure of triangle and square is missing; one being merged into another. The violet speaks of too early soul responsibility. (When Harry was three, a crippled brother was born). The lack of smoke shows that the will forces are not fully engaged in the metabolism.

The figure is higher off the earth than the tree, but it is three-folded. The blue-green has temperament connotations. The red head suggests his activity in the senses, and the gesture of the figure indicates a balance problem. The cutting-off of the sun in this manner, delineating it from the sky, always indicates a situation of jealousy.

The second picture (10 months later) shows a big change. The tree is a tree and earthed. The figure is sturdy and on the ground. The colour shows that he has come out of the temperament and into the weight of the physical body, and is inwardly tackling his problems. The dog (a more grounded intelligence) is leading the man to a newly-enlivened house over which a vermilion sun shines.

Conclusion

In such pictures we can find many more nuances which correlate with the child's character and development*. An assessment, showing whether or not the developmental phases of the first seven years are arrested, forms an important and vital contribution to our child study. Arrested development is a fundamental factor in children with learning problems, and should be remedied *before* any direct, tutorial coaching is given. The object of Extra Lesson Work is that any necessary, subsequent coaching can be received on the basis of a sound physiological and soul development.

EYE COLOUR AFFINITY DRAWINGS

Four examples of the process of adjustment of the Eye Colour Affinity during remediation, in this case over a two-year period, are shown on page 81.

---

*see *Sleep* by the author

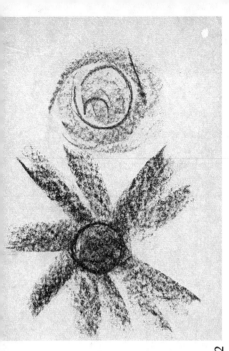

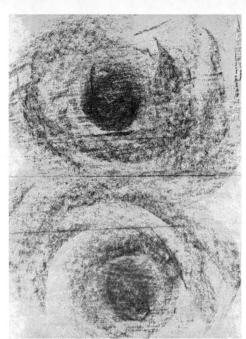

1

2

3

4

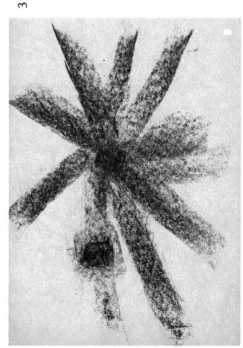

81

Examples of Flower-Rod Drawings

These are done from memory, i.e. third stage of exercise by assorted ages from 8½ years. They show the stress which children's perceptual organisation is under in relation to archetypal (building) forms.

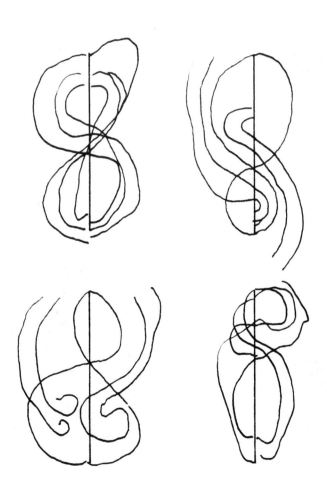

Balancing Lemniscates

Note: Draw very large, horizontally or vertically. The swing of the movement, and crossing points in a straight line, are the most important elements of this exercise. *Begin the vertical form at the top (x),* moving down the left hand side (in the direction of the arrow). Begin with the outermost loop.

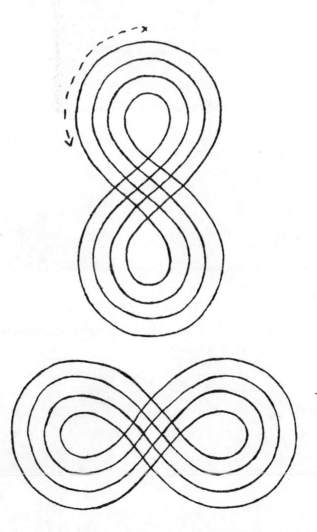

Example of the Secondary Colour Exercise, page 50

(painting strokes always from left to right)

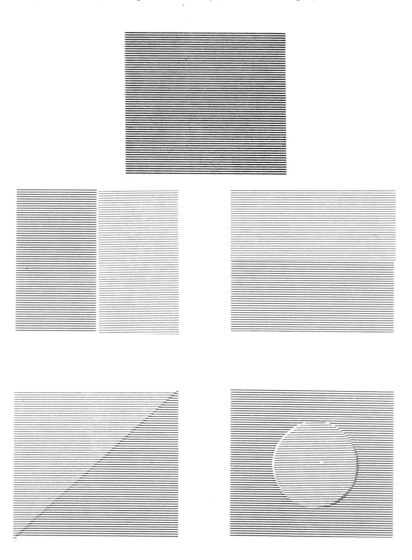

Triangle and Counting Forms

In Large Freehand Drawings

Interpenetrating Triangles

Expanding-Contracting Triangles

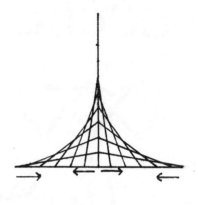

Counting Triangle

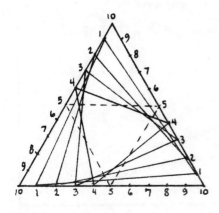

Counting Star

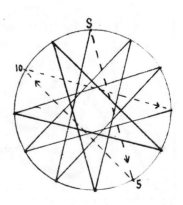

Types of Patterns

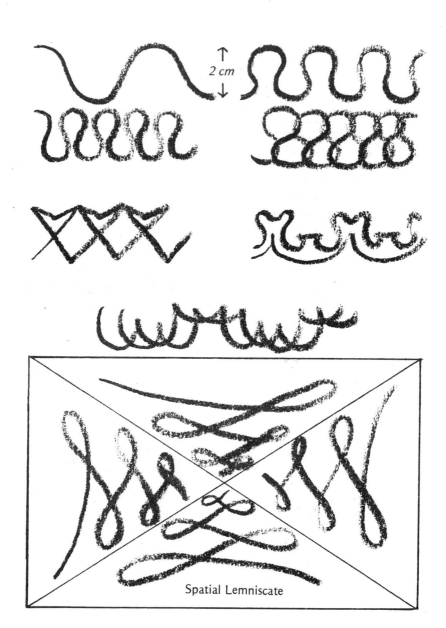

2 cm

Spatial Lemniscate

86

Mirror and Area Forms

Note: Teacher ——— *; Pupil* ------

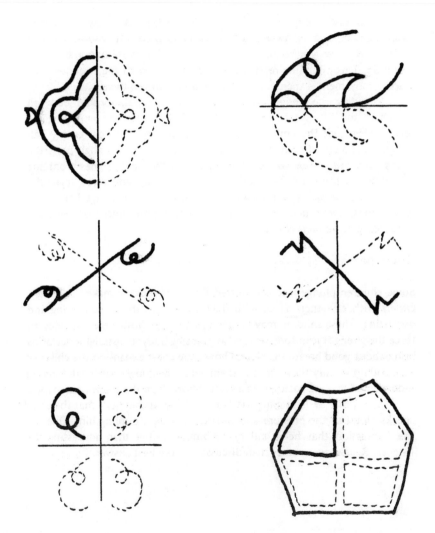

MAKING A LOAF OF BREAD

The preparation of the dough calls for practical use of reading and arithmetic, though if it is done in the first terms the instructions are given verbally; which is good practice for hearing and conceptualising, as these are invariably poor.

Show your pupil where everything is kept once only, even if it means opening every drawer and cupboard in subsequent lessons. You can always play "now you're hot — now you're cold" if the situation becomes desperate. This discipline reveals what has happened to the experience of space — movement — memory, and will help to enliven them.

Kneading the dough calls on a harmonious relationship between stretching and lifting movements with a spiral movement completing the activity. See that the child stands with his feet apart, weight evenly balanced, arms fully stretched and straight. With thumbs parallel, press the hands into the dough so that the weight of the body comes from the shoulders on to them. The dough is pressed down and away from the body. Using the palms of the hands and fingers, roll the dough back, turn in the ends, and round the dough with a spiral movement of the right hand. Repeat. *No bent elbows.*

Observations

Some children plunge into the wetted flour and quickly make the dough. Others withdraw their hands with flour sticking to them, exclaiming and protesting. These children may take longer to help. Notice the tendency to force the strength into forearms and avoid using body; the straightened arms bring about good breathing. Notice how little chest expansion the children have and how easily they tire. Let them enjoy the dough, patting it, flinging it down, and making patterns, faces, etc. Show them the traditional shapes.

It is while he is shaping the loaf, or busy kneading it, that the child speaks aloud of the pressure and worries that are troubling him. One has the impression that he is talking to himself rather than addressing the listener. Reassurance rather than discussion is the best answer.

BIBLIOGRAPHY

[O/P] following a reference denotes that the publication is out-of-print.

AS AN INTRODUCTION TO RUDOLF STEINER'S CONCEPTS
(all by Rudolf Steiner)

Practical Training in Thinking. (Lecture, 18.1.1909), Rudolf Steiner Press, London.

The Education of the Child in the Light of Anthroposophy. (Essay 1909), Rudolf Steiner Press, London.

The Four Temperaments. (Lecture 4.3.1909), Anthroposophic Press Inc., New York.

Philosophy, Cosmology and Religion. (10 lectures 6 — 15.9.1922), Anthroposophical Press Inc., New York, 1984.

LECTURES ON WHICH THIS BOOK IS BASED
(all by Rudolf Steiner)

The Wisdom of Man, of the Soul and of the Spirit. Anthroposophy, Psychosophy, Pneumatosophy. (12 lectures: 23 — 27.10.1909; 1 — 4.11.1910; 12 — 16.12.1911), Anthroposophic Press Inc., New York. [O/P].

The World as the Working of the Product of Balance. (3 lectures, 20 — 22.11.1914), Rudolf Steiner Press, London.

Die Sinneszone als eine Art Fortsetzung der Aussenwelt deren objektive Seite im Universum. Published in *"Mysterienwahrheiten und Weinachtsimpulse. Alte Mythen und ihre Bedeutung".* (Lecture 6, 30.12.1917). Rudolf Steiner Verlag, Dornach.

Meditatively Acquired Knowledge of Man. (4 lectures, 15,16,21,22.9.1920), Steiner Schools Fellowship Publications, Forest Row, Sussex, U.K.

Die Gestaltung des Moralisch-Geistigen des Menschen im Schlafe. (12 and 13.11.1921). Published in *Anthroposophie als Kosmosophie.* Zeiter Teil. "Die Gestaltung des Menschen als Ergebnis Kosmicher Wirkungen", Rudolf Steiner Verlag, Dornach, 1972.

REFERENCE BOOKS

Ablewhite, R.C. *The Slow Reader.* Heinemann. [O/P].

Aeppli, W. *The Care and Development of the Human Senses.* Steiner Schools Fellowship Publications, Forest Row, Sussex, U.K.

Ayres, J. J. *Sensory Development and the Child.* Western Psychology Services, Los Angeles, 1983.

Crosby, R. M. *Reading and the Dyslexic Child.* Souvenir Press, London. [O/P].

Diringer, D. *Writing — a Study of its Historical Evolution.* Thames & Hudson, London. [O/P].

Glas, N. *The Fulfilment of Old Age.* Anthroposophic Press Inc., New York. [O/P].

Jordan, D. *Dyslexia in the Classroom.* Charles Merril, Columbus, Ohio, U.S.A.

Johnson, D. L., & Myklebust, H. R. *Learning Disabilities.* Grune & Stratton, London. [O/P].

Kalinger, G., & Heil, C. L. *Basic Symmetry and Balance.* (Their relationship to perceptual Motor Development). Shippensburg State College, Penn. (Division of Special Services), Carlisle, Penn., U.S.A., 1972.

König, K. *The First Three Years of the Child.* Floris Books, Edinburgh, 1984.

Lehrs, E. *Man or Matter. An Introduction to a Spiritual Understanding of Nature on the Basis of Goethe's Method of Training, Observation and Thought.* Rudolf Steiner Press, London, May 1985.

SUPPLEMENTARY READING

Axline, V. M. *Dibs: In Search of Self.* Gollancz & Penguin, London, 1971.

Brown, C. *My Left Foot.* Secker, London. [O/P].

Frommer, E. *The Voyage through Childhood into the Adult World. A Description of Child Development.* Pergamon Press, Oxford, 1969.

Harwood, A. C. *The Recovery of Man in Childhood. A Study in the Educational Work of Rudolf Steiner.* Anthroposophic Press Inc., New York.

Hunt, J. *Move in Time.* (Pre-eurythmy exercises for classes and individuals). Take Time Products, Eastbourne, U.K., 1983.

Kalinger, G., & Kolson, C. *Reading and Learning Disabilities.* Charles Merril, Columbus, Ohio, U.S.A., 1969.

König, K. *Brothers and Sisters — A Study in Child Psychology.* Floris Books, Edinburgh.

Marshall, S. *An Experiment in Education.* Cambridge University Press, Cambridge, 1966.

Nash-Wortham, E. (Ed.). *Take Time.* (Exercises in co-ordination, rhythm and timing for children with specific difficulties related to language). Take Time Products, Eastbourne, U.K., 1979.

Pouderoyen, E. (Ed.). *Eurythmy.* (A collection of articles about eurythmy with photographs and diagrams). The Eurythmy Association of Southern California, Los Angeles, U.S.A.

Raffee, M. (et al). *Eurythmy and the Impulse of Dance with Sketches of Eurythmy Figures by Rudolf Steiner.* Rudolf Steiner Press, London, 1974.

Smith, S. *No Easy Answers. The Learning Disabled Child at Home and at School.* Bantam Books, London, 1980.

Steiner, R. *Eurythmy as Visible Speech.* (15 lectures, 24.6 — 12.7.1924). Rudolf Steiner Press, London, 1985.

Steiner, R. *The Kingdom of Childhood.* (7 lectures, 12 — 20.7.1924). Rudolf Steiner Press, London.

Strauss, M. *Understanding Children's Drawings. The Path to Manhood.* Rudolf Steiner Press, London, 1978.

Warner, S. A. *Teacher.* Penguin Books, London, 1980.

SOME TEACHING MATERIAL

Clausen, A. U., & Riedel, M. *Zeichnen-Sehen Lernen.* (Form and pattern drawing — visual, little reading matter). F. Ch. Mellinger Verlag, Stuttgart.

Colum, P. *The King of Ireland's Son.* Floris Books, Edinburgh, 1984.

Colum, P. *Myths of the World.* Grosset & Dunlap, New York.

Schonell, F. J. *Essentials in Teaching and Testing Spelling.* MacMillan, London.

Skipper, M. *The Meeting Pool.* (Especially suitable for older children to make their own endings to the stories; suitable reading for all ages). Penguin, London. [O/P].

INDEX

94

OTHER BOOKS BY THE AUTHOR

TEACHING CHILDREN TO WRITE: Its connection with the development of spatial consciousness in the child.

Miss McAllen describes the viewpoint of Steiner education in the teaching of the art of handwriting to the young child so that reading arises out of this activity as a matter of course. The book covers the Class Teacher's needs through to Class 6, demonstrating how the movement patterns in letter formation reflect the activity involving the total movement organisation of the child. If we lose the capacity of handwriting, as is a possibility today, we lose something basic in our evolution as human beings.

SLEEP: An unobserved element in Education.

Here are presented the main aspects of Rudolf Steiner's spiritual research on the experiences of the soul during sleep. These facts give insight into the pedagogical principles of Waldorf education and are of concern to teachers in Steiner schools as well as students of Anthroposophy.